AS SHE IS DYING

Kevin Cain

ELM HILL

A Division of
HarperCollins Christian Publishing

www.elmhillbooks.com

As She Is Dying

Published in Nashville, Tennessee, by Elm Hill, an imprint of Thomas Nelson. Elm Hill and Thomas Nelson are registered trademarks of HarperCollins Christian Publishing, Inc.

Elm Hill titles may be purchased in bulk for educational, business, fund-raising, or sales promotional use. For information, please e-mail SpecialMarkets@ ThomasNelson.com.

All Scripture quotations, unless otherwise indicated, are taken from the New American Standard Bible˚. Copyright © 1960, 1962, 1963, 1968, 1971, 1972, 1973, 1975, 1977, 1995 by The Lockman Foundation. Used by permission. (www.Lockman.org)

"Breathe On Me" by Lucy Fisher
Copyright© 1998 Hillsong Music Publishing (APRA) (adm. in the US and Canada at CapitolCMGPublishing.com)
All rights reserved. Used by permission.
International Copyright Secured. All Rights Reserved. Used by Permission.

"Needle. Fall Down" by Charles Wesley Godwin
Used by permission.

"Redwoods & Daisies" by Jason Upton
Used by permission.

Library of Congress Cataloging-in-Publication Data

Library of Congress Control Number: 2018955482

ISBN 978-1-595559166 (Paperback)
ISBN 978-1-595559180 (Hardbound)
ISBN 978-1-595559135 (eBook)

For

Lesley, Tanner, Garrett, and Cameron

As She Is Dying

I ask her sons and daughters,
"When is she most beautiful?"
Those who love her answer,
"As she is dying."

I see her now.
She offers light of red,
And orange,
And gold.

CONTENTS

ACKNOWLEDGMENTS

This book would never have been written were it not for the encouragement of a group of Christian musicians, poets, artists, and worshippers with whom I attended a silent retreat at the Jesuit Retreat House on Lake Winnebago during the winter of 2017. After four days in absolute silence we headed back to the home of our retreat organizer, Christian artist Jason Upton. While in Jason's recording studio, appropriately named *The Hog Shed*, we took our culminating step as brothers as we celebrated Holy Communion for nearly four hours. It was one of the most amazing times of spirit and truth worship I have ever experienced. All of us lost track of the time.

While all worshipping in the Spirit, two members of our newly solidified brotherhood, Pat Barrett and Ben Smith, saw that they had less than an hour to catch their return flight. Eight of us piled into an SUV and, with Jason driving, sped off to the airport.

On the way Jason said, "Pastor Kevin, did you bring your journal with you?" I told him I had, and he said, "Read us the words you read to us during the Holy Communion service."

I was surprised. The gentlemen I had come to know for the first time over the last few days were all well-known Christian artists. I was sitting among them as an Appalachian pastor from Westover, West Virginia. Surely, these polished spiritual poets wouldn't want to hear my words again. With their encouragement, I began to read the piece with which I had opened up our afternoon Holy Communion service.

I read it once, and Jason said, "Read it again."

I read it again, and Jason said, "Read it again."

I read it a third time, and Jason said, "Read it again."

With the fourth request for my work to be read, another of the brotherhood, Micah Lother, said, "Wait. Wait. Wait. Here, plug my iPhone in. We need music with it this time."

I believed them to be potentially joking with me.

With movie score instrumentation filling the SUV, Jason said a final time, "Read it again."

With hesitation in my voice, I read the piece one final time.

Whoever was sitting in the front passenger seat turned off the music, and no one said a word. I didn't know whether I should expect laughter or applause. Then Jason broke the silence, saying, "Kev, you're a writer. You need to write." Then and there I decided to surrender to God using me in this art form.

I want to thank the brothers in that SUV who encouraged me: Pat Barrett, Ben Smith, Andrew Ehrenzeller, Micah Lother, Daniel Dauwe, Lambert Dekkers, and Jason Upton. I want to especially thank Jason. Only with his love and encouragement has *As She Is Dying* become a reality.

I also want to thank my fellow pastors and staff members of *Kingdom, A Community Church,* with special thanks going to Leslie Brooks and Jim Yohn for all their help with administrative tasks and editing.

I want to thank Pastor Bryan Loritts and Pat Barrett for their endorsements and support.

Seth Gartin designed a beautiful cover that captures the heart of *As She Is Dying*'s message—many thanks. Thank you to Jenny Secreto for her edits, and Jane Haines, Ryan Stuart, and Tim Linkous for your efforts at the most foundational of levels.

I want to thank Linda Tomkowski, Sharon Chapman, and Byron Nelson for not allowing me to stop putting pen to paper. Thanks also go to Bill McCulla for teaching me the kindness and compassion necessary to properly love and serve grieving families, along with each and every funeral director with whom I have had the pleasure of working.

Gratitude goes to every one of the nearly 1,000 families who have granted me the honor of eulogizing and laying to rest their loved ones. It has been my privilege to serve you.

And, above all, to Lesley, Tanner, Garrett, and Cameron, those with whom God has blessed me as flesh of flesh, bone of bone. I am eternally grateful for you.

K. B. C.

A Brief Introduction:
My Story of Appalachian Eulogies

"The eulogy, or 'funeral praise,' is the oldest and, in some ways, least valued of our literary forms. It is practiced by amateurs. When some-one dies, it is customary for a member of the family or a friend to 'say a few words,' composed under great duress, about the deceased. Mourners are not literary critics; we will accept any words at all, as long as they are not mean-spirited or self-serving, and a particularly moving or graceful tribute is delivered, we are grateful for the balm."

Phyllis Theroux, <u>The Book of Eulogies</u>

I'm an Appalachian preacher.

I'm not sure I always have been, but I know I always will be.

I was only sixteen years old when I preached my first sermon, and I was but twenty years old when I served my first four rural Appalachian churches: Glover Gap, Metz, Rymer, and Logansport. The four were located in the suburbs of Mannington, West Virginia (Population 2,059), and were part of the West Marion Charge, of the Fairmont District, of the West Virginia United Methodist Church. Sadly, local little country congregations are typically the staging grounds for young pastors looking to things bigger and better; or they are settings of pulpit supply where Hell's fire and brimstone enter and exit weekly through the revolving door of the sacred desk; or they are final resting grounds for reverends of retirement age. Yet I began as a Pollyanna preacher. I never saw the hills and hollers of West Virginia churches as anything but home. Somehow I believed I would be the preacher to these folks forever. Known or not, preaching is in my blood.

My maternal grandmother was the daughter of one of West Virginia's original circuit-riding preachers. His eulogy had long been offered before my arrival, but I am told my great-grandfather had eleven churches, and Sunday after Sunday he rode on horseback from church to church to church to church, and so on. His daughter, my grandmother, and her daughter, my mother, taught me how to be a preacher. I say *preacher* because that is who the minister always was. Growing up in small-town Appalachia, and even now, *reverend* is out of reach and *pastor* is a big title found in the evangelicalism of cities. I cannot remember anyone ever calling a minister Pastor Hugh, or Pastor Charles, or Pastor Chester. In my home church, there was one man on a spiritual pedestal, called Reverend Kerr, but he was spoken of more in hushed tones. He was a sort of Christian version of John Henry, or Paul Bunyan, or Davey Crockett. No one could ever measure up to him, so before and after him the minister was simply called *Preacher*.

As I said, my granny and my mom taught me how to be one.

Before I headed to Mannington, my grandmother and mom sat me down and told me what good preachers do and don't do. I said to them, "You know, I know the Bible pretty well and I preach a decent sermon. I don't mind visiting people in the nursing homes and hospitals, and I especially like kids and old people. I'm young enough to relate to teenagers and the oldsters will see me as someone they can mold. I'm okay with sitting in the backseat, even when it isn't my seat to sit in. There's just one thing I don't know how to do: *What do I say when someone dies?"*

With that question I began my odyssey into the calling I had no desire to ever enter. Then and there, I began a life that would become funeral after funeral, sadness after sadness, celebration after celebration, a whole lot of tears sprinkled with an occasional remembrance of laughter.

My granny said, "Honey, let me tell you a story:

There was once a little grade school girl who was the prize of any set of parents. She was loving, and caring, and did her home-work and her chores. She brushed her teeth, and she always said please and thank you, so when she was late coming home from school one day her mother became worried. An hour passed and then two. At first her mother thought perhaps she was playing, but as the third hour approached and the streetlight came on, the mother knew something was wrong. She reached for the phone to call the police. As she dialed the first number, her little girl walked through the kitchen door.

'Where have you been?' the mother questioned. 'I was wor-ried about you.'

Unshaken herself, the little girl eased her mother's fears as she began to recount the reason for her lateness.

'Mother,' she said, 'you remember my friend, Nancy.'

Patiently, the mother shook her head.

'Well, Mother, Nancy had the most beautiful china doll. We played with her all day at school, and on the school bus the entire way home. As we were getting off the bus at our stop, Nancy dropped her doll and she broke into pieces.'

Now proud, rather than angry, the mother said, 'Oh, I under-stand. You stayed and helped Nancy put her doll back together again.'

The little girl shook her head, saying, 'No, Mother ... the doll couldn't be repaired. I just stayed and helped Nancy cry.'

"Honey, being a preacher is about preaching and teaching the Bible, visiting, and relating. But a great deal of the time, you are going to have to help people cry. Let their tears be the balm for their souls; and, while they're crying, maybe help them to laugh a little. When someone is crying, remembering and laughing won't make it go completely away, but it will help. These are two of our greatest gifts: *tears and laughter.*"

And that is how my life as preacher of local Appalachian churches and the eulogies of the people began. Like my life in the pulpit, that day the conversation with my grandmother and mother continued. The two reminded me of a few more things necessary for helping people work through their funeral day grief.

They told me to say the person's name. Too often pastors officiating funerals read through their canned funeral service, or they talk more about the platitudes of death and life than they do the person they are there to eulogize. And when they do get around to speaking about the person, they choose to use *he* and *she* and *him* and *her*, rather than saying the name of the deceased. There is solace in saying someone's name. If the person's name can be said, somehow the deceased seems to comfortingly linger.

Next, I was never to pretend to know a person I did not know. Very often, families have no church affiliation, and while many believe we have become a post-Christian society, most Appalachians still view having a preacher around for marriages and funerals as a necessity. In cases where a loved one has died and a family doesn't have a preacher, the staff of the local funeral home will attempt to provide one. I have been a resident of Westover, West Virginia, for all but eighteen months of my nearly half-century of existence. My grandfather was Mayor of Westover. My grandmother, father, and I have served on Westover City Council. My father was a local small business owner and, since the 1960s within the local school system, four members of my family have been school teachers and administrators. I am now a preacher in the town where I was born, bred, and raised. After that résumé, one would think I would know everyone in my version of Mayberry. I do not. Still I have become one of this community's preachers, and my roots are deep, so funeral requests for people I do not know often arise. I officiate between thirty-five and fifty funerals annually, and have done so since my late twenties. The number of funerals I have officiated is somewhere between 750–1,000. It is impossible to know everyone I have been asked to lay to rest. If I do not know the person, I do not pretend to. At the beginning of a funeral, it is a simple and polite thing to say, "I never had the opportunity to know ...." In the midst of grief, over masquerade, it is honesty that is preferred.

There were many more lessons provided that day, but the one that has proven most helpful is to simply ask the family what they would like shared concerning the deceased. The process I follow is quite simple. The typical funeral tradition of Appalachia is to have one day of viewing the deceased's body and the next day a funeral service. Those closest to the deceased typically arrive at the funeral home one hour prior to the time of viewing. I am there when they arrive but keep myself unseen. They are ushered into the room where the casket holding the deceased's body rests. I allow them to spend their time. Then, once they have collected themselves, I enter, sit with them, and make a simple statement, saying, "I don't want you to walk out of here tomorrow saying, 'I wish Kevin would have said *this*.' You tell me the *this* and I will put it all together for you." My journal is out, and I am prepared to write. Usually there is silence. It is a silence that is necessary and must be allowed to run its course. Then comes the *this* from the loved ones. Sometimes it is a lot. Sometimes it is a little. Sometimes it is already written out for me. Sometimes they say nothing at all—those are the hardest. Still when the *this* is given, honor can begin to be brought to the God Who reconciles us, and tribute can be brought to the one we will come together to remember. Most certainly during every service, either blatantly or subtly, I share Christ's reconciling Gospel. Yet a funeral is no time for institutional platitudes. Every funeral should simply honor God, bring tribute to the deceased, and be an offering of hope to those who remain.

During this time of preparation for the day we say goodbye, not even one time have families asked me to reconcile their deceased loved one to God through eulogy. They already assume the person to be in heaven. And if they think Hell to be the person's lot, they do not say. Most assume the golden rule for eternity's placement, and most believe the deceased has achieved the eternal commendation. But to be honest, after all these years of ministry, I'm not sure any really think about eternal standing very much at all. They assume eternal standing as a result of a passive and unvetted theology. As a result, much of what I do is bring hope to a moment that, for them, is bathed in finality. This leaves me with the responsibility of truth telling. I must tell the truth about the individual— the obvious good and bad—while offering hope. I must tell the truth of the Gospel's necessity for salvation. I must tell the truth about present grief and being defined by this one we have lost.

I believe in Heaven.

I believe in Hell.

Yet God has never consulted me about any individual's eternal standing. In the funerals I officiate and the eulogies I write, I will say "Heaven" when confession of Christ by the individual and spiritual fruit bearing is easily discerned but, as you will soon see, instead of damning an individual, I close every funeral by asking for the peace and blessing of our God to be upon the deceased and those at the place of funeral who are there to grieve and pay tribute.

Eternal standing is not up to me.

Paul speaks of reconciliation of creation to the Church at Colossae, saying, "For it was the Father's good pleasure for all the fullness to dwell in Him, and through Him to reconcile all things to Himself, having made peace through the blood of His cross; through Him, I say, whether things on earth or things in heaven." (Colossians 1:19, 20 NASB) And if that weren't enough, Paul continues his statement of hope for reconciliation, saying, "When you were dead in your transgressions and the uncircumcision of your flesh, He made you alive together with Him, having forgiven us all our transgressions, having canceled out the certificate of debt consisting of decrees against us, which was hostile to us; and He has taken it out of the way, having nailed it to the cross." (Colossians 2:13, 14 NASB)

As a preacher, it is not my responsibility to reconcile anyone. I share the Gospel of the Reconciler, and when an individual has passed on, be the person a member of the institution of Christianity or not, I do my very best to find evidence of the reconciled life. When I cannot, I simply speak of the individual's greatness and compassionately offer the Gospel's hope of reconciliation.

The longer I live, the more I come to find that I know little of the God I know so well. Like Abraham alongside God, before a people who seem to be most worthy of perishing, I say, "Far be it from You to do such a thing, to slay the righteous with the wicked, so that the righteous and the wicked are treated alike. Far be it from You! Shall not the Judge of all the earth deal justly?" (Genesis 18:25 NASB) I have given my life to bring hope to a people who have little reason to hope. I have heard some say, "If West Virginia is almost Heaven, then can we at least first see what Hell is like?" Perhaps this is true. Maybe we have allowed our hills' majesty and grandeur to blind us from coal dust and addiction. Yet, I do see hope. I see hope in what is dying. I see hope in what is dead. I see hope in what remains. Yes, death has the keen ability to either clear up, cover up, or stir up. Still sometimes we must descend in order to turn into the clouds.

This is a book about death that offers stories of life. After officiating so many funerals, much has been learned as I've stood at death's door and mourned loss with those who still love those now gone.

Isn't it funny how genuine love is never past tense?

So, in these pages, you will find a little bit of wisdom, some stories of hope, and the eulogizing words of my mouth and the meditations of my heart, which I trust have been acceptable in the sight of my strength and my Redeemer.

Somehow and somewhere in death, hope must be discovered. Maybe, through the literal metaphor of Appalachians' deaths, you can see life.

Some were reconciled long before their deaths.

Some were reconciled just prior to their deaths.

And others were reconciled in the midst of death.

There is hope for all ... hope's breath, even in death.

A LITTLE BIT OF WISDOM

CHAPTER I

THEY NEVER CLOSE FAIRMONT ROAD:

GETTING BACK ON THE CAROUSEL

OF LIFE

The funeral home where I officiate most of my funerals is adjacent to Fairmont Road. Now, Fairmont Road is no Route 66, nor is it comparable to the I-95 corridor, and it certainly is but a thread in comparison to the lanes upon lanes encircling Atlanta. Yet for little ol' Westover, West Virginia, it is our city's only major thoroughfare. It runs from Exit 152 of I-79 all the way to the Westover Bridge that links the west side of the Monongahela River to the east side. Nearly thirty times a year I find myself inside that Fairmont Road-adjacent-funeral-home officiating funeral services. After all these years with all these families and all these circumstances, illnesses and ages associated with death, there is one constant between the funeral home and Fairmont Road: *When a person dies, the powers that be never close Fairmont Road.* For the families inside the funeral home, everything has come to a dead stop. For the people going up and down Fairmont Road, life doesn't even slow down. Very few people pause for the death of those they do not know. Society and the speed and volume with which it travels does not suffer fools, and it certainly does not pause to acknowledge the dead nor the paralyzing grief of those mourning. In the midst of mortality, life moves both along and on. How are those closest to the deceased ever to merge once again onto life's Fairmont Roads and rejoin the carousel of life?

I'm not sure people inside the funeral home even realize the road outside is still there until the funeral concludes and they emerge from the funeral home with the preacher leading the way and pallbearers carrying the casket down the steps to the black funeral coach whose back hatch waits to receive the vessel that holds the body of the deceased. There is a somberness about those moments, and depending on how closely individuals sat towards the front of the funeral chapel during the service now determines how soon their conversations start and some long-awaited cigarettes are lit. The family and closest friends of the deceased shuffle to their cars with little to no thought as to how they are going to stumble back into life, while the less affected gaze at their watches and consider their least obstructed getaway back to life's quick pace and desired noise. Not everyone who is part of the funeral has signed up to be part of the funeral procession. Those who passed the casket first inside are typically those who drive off first outside.

Life and Fairmont Road is calling.

I always find it interesting that once the funeral procession is about to break the imaginary seal between the funeral home property and Fairmont Road, the traffic on Fairmont Road does not stop, nor does it even politely slow. If anything, when the purple lights atop the funeral coach begin to shine, the cars speed up rather than slow down. There's always a mall, or a gas station, or a home supply store, or a restaurant to get to. Usually there is police escort, and usually a funeral home employee has to risk his own life as he steps into traffic with a hand raised to stop the unlucky cars that did not make it past the funeral home soon enough. This is not the whining cynicism of a curmudgeon. Sadly, it is the sad reality of a selfish world.

The journey to the cemetery is equally frustrating. At each intersection along the route, the funeral director and the preacher who sit in the funeral coach's driver's seat and passenger seat, respectively, must hold their hands up to the window in order for traffic to slow and come to a stop. Certainly, those who speed to make it out before the funeral procession reaches them will be the same ones who will curse the speeding cars on the day their loved ones are laid to rest.

Life and Fairmont Road never closes.

If the funeral and the funeral procession is a holding of one's breath, then reaching the cemetery is to be considered exhaling.

The people stop behind the hearse.

The pallbearers carry the casket to the graveside.

The preacher offers the committal service.

The funeral home employee says, "This concludes our services. You may now return to your cars."

What began a few days ago with the expiration of breath is now over. There is no longer liberty to be without breath. Life must begin again. How are those closest to the deceased ever to merge once again onto life's Fairmont Roads and rejoin the carousel of life?

Years ago I was called upon to perform the funeral service for a woman named Ruby. She and her husband Joe had been married for sixty-three years. He was a World War II veteran, and while Joe was away fighting against tyranny, Ruby signed up to be one of this country's riveting Rosies.

And now the riveter was no more.

The funeral home was empty except for Joe and Ruby's grown son and his wife, and Joe. Very much to the side, I and the father of the funeral director looked on as we granted the three their last few moments before they would leave and Ruby's casket would be closed.

Joe was no longer a young, fighting soldier. He was a gray-haired man who was confined to a wheelchair. I remember Joe's son walked behind the wheelchair with his hands on the handles, but he wasn't pushing. Joe was digging his heels into the carpet and was literally drawing his own wheelchair across the floor, foot pull by foot pull. Tears were streaming down his cheeks, and his nose was in need of a handkerchief. It was a sight of absolute love and absolute loss.

Joe could barely see over the edge of the coffin, yet he looked at Ruby without pause. Joe lifted his hand and placed it squarely over Ruby's.

How long was that moment?

In the midst of it, the funeral director's father whispered to me, saying, "How do you go on?"

Before I could answer the whispering question that had been left in my ear, Joe patted Ruby's hand and said, "I'll see you soon."

I whispered back, "That's how you go on."

Joe died within the year.

Love is one of few things that perfects during times of pause. Love grows as it is filtered through grief. Love grows as it waits for reunion. Love grows as it has nothing to feed on but memories and tears and laughter. It is a bad thing to be constantly gratified. The impatience of the world leaves speeding and blaring society nothing to look forward to. Those who interrupt and selfishly advance are those who are most deeply infected by death's dissection. Yet when a life loves fully and looks forward fully, the speed and volume of life can neither seduce nor deny.

In the midst of loss and greatest grief, slow down and consider. Are you one who believes in something or nothing to come? If it's nothing, then why spend your days grieving until nothing comes? If it's something, then celebrate the achievements while living this absence, and look forward to the perfect fullness of that which is yet to come.

Anyone can speed by. Anyone can ignore. Anyone can cut off or hurry those along, so he can get where he wants to go. Such is the cheap and generic life.

It is a good thing to pause as the world speeds by. It is a good thing to mourn. It is a good thing to pay respect. It is a good thing to remember, to wait, and to live with the hope of seeing soon those we love.

How are those closest to the deceased ever to merge once again onto life's Fairmont Roads and rejoin the carousel of life?

We simply rise every day and with our heels pull ourselves across the carpet, gaze into the eyes of the past, wipe our tears and our noses, pat the hands of our loved ones, and say, "I'll see you soon."

CHAPTER II

DEFINED BY THOSE WE HAVE LOST

By September 9, 2000, I had been preaching the Gospel for fourteen years.

September 9 is my birthday, and on my first birthday of the new millennia, my always educating schoolteacher mother bought me a textbook of sorts. My present from her was *The Book of Eulogies,* edited with commentary by Phyllis Theroux. Inside the front cover my mother wrote these words:

Dear Kevin,

You've always seemed to find the right words to eulogize family and friends that bring comforting and joyful memories to those who are grieving. Maybe this book can make your future tasks easier.

Remember at my funeral to have the Koon family (a long-standing Appalachian family singing group) sing "Lighthouse" and "What a Day." I would also like a soloist to sing, "If You Could See Me Now." Everyone should sing "Jesus Keep Me Near the Cross."

—Mom

I have grown to understand the need to think about life without one's parents. Initially it is a thought that is much avoided, but over time when faith is sound and we are transformed into those who grieve with hope, the reality of absence is more easily swallowed.

I will miss them.

Hopefully, they won't have to miss me first.

My mother was a bit prophetic. The 400-page birthday present did make my future tasks easier. Theroux's compilation of eulogies, commentaries, epitaphs, and poetry continue to scour the dirty feet of my surrendered heart. Thank goodness, because my calling to minister through eulogy has never lessened. With the growing demand of more and more funerals upon me, the greatest lesson learned from this birthday gift are words from then *New York Times* editorial columnist, Anna Quindlen. Quindlen's editorial was titled, *The Living Are Defined By Whom They Have Lost*, and according to Theroux, Quindlen's column received more reader mail than any other she had ever written. Two sections from the editorial will forever shape my approach to funerals.

The first:

> *Grief remains one of the few things that has the power to silence us. It is a whisper in the world and a clamor within. More than sex, more than faith, even more than its usher death, grief is unspoken, publicly ignored except for those moments at the funeral that are over too quickly, or the conversations among the cognoscenti, those of us who recognize in one another a kindred chasm deep in the center of who we are.*

The second:

> *The landscapes of all our lives become as full of craters as the surface of the moon ... I write my obituaries carefully and think*

about how little the facts suffice, not only to describe the dead but
to tell what they will mean to the living all the rest of our lives.
We are defined by whom we have lost.

When one who has defined us is gone, we grieve. When grief just lies there as a freshly dug, freshly covered, six-foot-hole, it is difficult to live as one who has been defined. And there the preacher stands looking at a graveside full of people who are broken, and he knows he must tell them that at some point they must merge from this stop of unrestful rest in order to rejoin life. Life and grief are two of the things to which we cling most tightly.

Regardless of the hill or holler, everyone knows harvest is always a product of the seeds planted during the final days of winter's death. Only those who are committed to hunger bemoan the sower who sows seed into freshly overturned, cold ground. So, in the setting of visitation, funeral, eulogy, and committal, someone must assume the role of sower or else most will grasp for the life already gone and cling to the grief they never want to release.

Grief has a right to life, and it must be allowed to live. After grief has lived, it must equally be allowed to die—a dying some call death's death. Still, during grief's life cycle, the grieving must acknowledge how they have been defined by the one whose loss they are mourning. Acknowledged definition permits grief to be an agent of both healing and propulsion. We heal, and compassion is birthed where grief once stood. Grief's remembrances propel us towards definition and new days. New days, where the defined can now continue with defining, until the days when others will grieve and another preacher will say, "We are defined by those we have lost."

Life. Defining. Defined. Death. Grief. Healing. Propulsion. New days. Such is the necessary cycle that must continue until reconciliation is without foe.

TOO YOUNG TO BE DYIN'

I wonder how many times I have uttered the phrase, "Too young to be dyin'."

Burying parents' children is the most crushing ministry any preacher is ever called upon to do. No matter the words, they could not ease the pain of laying a child to rest. In the midst of the greatest agony, preachers are asked to bring a reconciling balm to a torment we most likely will never personally know. Yet we must. Through shoulders, arms, ears, and the abundance of our hearts, we must provide the compassionate compress to stop the flow of a bleeding heart.

I can remember as a child seeing in my grandparents' Morrison Avenue home a picture of a pretty, blonde-haired girl. She looked to be about eighteen, and she was wearing a light blue dress and pearls. I asked my granny to tell me who she was. Granny said, "That's Dorthy Ellen. She's our daughter. She died in a car crash when she was just a girl." Years later I learned the story of my aunt Dorthy Ellen's death. It's still too painful to share. To this day, my mother tells me that after the wreck my papaw should never have asked to see her. He was a brilliant man, but also an alcoholic. Liquor, not beer or wine. Seeing his daughter dead and in that bodily condition only made his interpretation of his own brilliance more futile and his alcoholism only worse. So, long before I was a preacher, death invited me to the gathering of those who had been hazed into the fraternity of parents forced to say, goodbye to their children.

It is important to once again hear that truth.

When you are not the parent you may feel pain, but it is not a parent's pain. Those who find themselves outside of parental anguish but inside the circumstance of childhood death, the best any person can do is through silent presence, wait to be asked to help.

And so I've tried.

During my sophomore year of high school, I took my first experiential steps towards childhood death's door. His name was Paul. He was the same age as my sister, Keely. I was two years younger than they were, but I had watched Keely go to school with Paul from Morgan Heights Kindergarten to Westover Elementary, Westover Elementary to Westover Junior High, Westover Junior High to Morgantown High School. They were seniors now, and they were finished with classes and just days away from graduation. Paul was always so nice. He reminded me of an oversized Winnie the Pooh, but his coloring was not oranges and reds; instead, he was blues and grays, like Eeyore. He was quiet and kind. I always liked Paul. Before he heard *Pomp and Circumstance* play, before he crossed the platform and transitioned his tassel from one side of his cap to the other, Paul drowned in the backwaters of Cheat Lake. If I remember correctly, he was trying to save his girlfriend from drowning. She died too. I never met his parents, nor did I meet hers. I know all four still hurt today.

I hadn't even made it out of high school when I met Sam, a little-leaguer at our local baseball park. He got cancer. My friends and I were teenage umpires and powerless to help. At that age, we couldn't even get the strike zone right. As dust-covered teenage umpires, how could we ever provide support to Sam's dad and mom? Sam died. I still see his dad from time to time. I still don't know what to say. He hasn't asked me to say anything yet but we always talk, and he is always kind.

At that same baseball park was a junior high kid named Jimmy. He was annoying and always around. We were eighteen. He was twelve.

Honestly he could have disappeared and we wouldn't have even noticed. But Jimmy kept asking me if he could umpire. Truth be told, I didn't know what I was doing any more than Jimmy, so putting him on a field to umpire the bases for six- and seven-year-olds couldn't do any harm. I don't think my buddies even noticed, but there Jimmy was in all his umpiring glory. A twelve-year-old with the big boys in the eighteen-year-old's umpire's office; Jimmy could not have been happier.

Well, we all retired from the baseball park after a couple more summers, and Jimmy took my job as field director of WESMON Little League. We were now in our twenties. Jimmy was now driving. He was diagnosed with cancer not long after. He fought and fought, but Jimmy died too. On the day of his funeral, I sat in the back of the room. His grandfather preached his funeral. There were so many people there. I just remember thinking, *How's Jimmy's grandfather getting through this?* Jimmy's grandfather was an old preacher from a backwoods church in Southern West Virginia. He held it together until he said his final "Amen." Then Preacher Phil turned into Jimmy's granddad once again. In tears, he collapsed into the arms of his family. Now as a preacher myself, I often find myself in the graveyard where Jimmy is buried. Every time I am in Arnettesville Cemetery, I stop at Jimmy's grave and pay my respects.

And so it goes. Deeper and deeper into ministry I travel. There are more and more, more and more. I just keep saying, "Too young to be dyin'."

My friend Billie got sick. She was admitted to the intensive care unit. I knelt by her bedside and said the exact same words Jesus said at the bedside of Jairus's daughter, "Talitha cum." Jairus's daughter was given back to her parents, alive. Not long after *I had called* for my little lamb to arise, I eulogized Billie. I love her parents, her brother, and her sisters. Billie's absence still lingers. Her daughter will graduate from high school this year. All those years ago, before I stood to offer Billie's eulogy, her sister, Lisa, stood beside Billie's casket and said to those sitting in the Woodland United Methodist Church sanctuary, "I know none of you know what to say to us, but thank you for trying to say something.

Even if it wasn't quite right, thank you for at least trying to bring us comfort." I do not remember anything that I said that day other than words of frustration and faith prayerfully spoken to God. Through many tears I prayed, "Lord, I am not happy about this, but I will not forsake You." My frustration and uncontrollable tears from that day will always pale in comparison to those of Billie's family.

> *"Have I not commanded you? Be strong and courageous! Do not tremble or be dismayed, for the Lord your God is with you wherever you go."*
>
> *(JOSHUA 1:9 NASB)*

God's words to Joshua after the death of Moses were the words we leaned upon when we eulogized Johnny Koon. Johnny was a fourteen-year-old kid in my congregation. I've known his family my entire life. Johnny also had cancer. He battled for years. On August 13, 2004, Johnny was a patient at the Pediatric Intensive Care Unit at West Virginia University's Ruby Memorial Hospital. That day Johnny was intubated. He remained so until March 4, 2005. On that late winter day with spring ready to birth once again, around Johnny's bedside in a makeshift basement bedroom in his parents' rented home, more than thirty of us were gathered. Johnny was leaving us. For nearly seven months, Johnny hadn't taken a breath without assistance. With no physical life remaining, Johnny's respiratory therapist removed his intubation tube. Then, all of a sudden, this lanky, scarecrow of a boy who had provided us so much life and inspiration gave us a miracle. Johnny never opened his eyes to look at us. On his own, Johnny breathed deeply through his nose and then exhaled through his mouth. That was Johnny's last breath before his first breath.

> *Breathe on me, breath of God*
> *Love and life that makes me free*
> *Breathe on me, breath of God*
> *Fan the flame within me,*

Teach my heart, heal my soul,
Speak the life, that in Christ we know
Take me to your sanctuary, breathe on me

(*Breathe On Me*, Hillsong United)

Once while standing with Johnny's mom at his PICU bedside, I attempted to provide her unsolicited comfort, saying, "I try to imagine sometimes...."

She stopped me immediately. "That is not your child lying there. Love your children where they are, and stand with us while we love Johnny where he is."

I received the lesson, and I hold it to this day. Each person's story is his own. Even in losing a child, the loss of a child holds no comparison. And when we've only held a child's life and not his death, it is better to just remain quiet and allow the one losing and those who have lost to lead the conversation.

"Too young to be dyin'."

My wife played college basketball. When her days of dribbling and shooting concluded, she moved on to coaching young children wanting to learn to be cagers. Soon my wife was coaching our sons. One of the little boys on her fifth-grade team didn't make it through the season. He died in a four-wheeler accident.

After his funeral concluded, from the front row the boy's mom stared at many of his classmates and teammates standing and looking down into her little boy's coffin.

The camaraderie of the casket is one children should never have to know, but far too many times I have seen kids huddled together, together looking down at a dead friend. They don't see a body. They just see a missing classmate, teammate, pal. Such is the next greatest tragedy. Typically and tragically, those schoolmates remember for a day and forget for a lifetime. It is a great difficulty for teenagers to grasp the truth of their own mortality.

To bury a child.

If the child is no longer a child but now an adult, and that adult dies before his parents, does the achievement of adulthood make death a lesser blow for the parents who remain? I watched my paternal grandmother mourn the loss of her fifty-plus-year-old daughter. My maternal grandmother laid to rest her fifty-eight-year-old son. At both funerals there were no less tears. When it is *your child* you are burying, age is insignificant. The child is your child, and fairness declares that you should have gone first.

Can the death of a child be reconciled?

Certainly there are answers, but the moral authority acquired in the loss of a child permits the mourning parents to approach reconciliation at their own pace. Knowing this, I have learned to not offer answers but the hope of peace.

As I searched for answers to give in preparation for my friend Billie's funeral, I stumbled across this hope of peace. It is offered by God through the prophet, Isaiah. God simply says this:

> *Seek the LORD while He may be found;*
> *Call upon Him while He is near.*
> *Let the wicked forsake his way*
> *And the unrighteous man his thoughts;*
> *And let him return to the LORD,*
> *And He will have compassion on him,*
> *And to our God,*
> *For He will abundantly pardon.*
> *"For My thoughts are not your thoughts,*
> *Nor are your ways My ways," declares the LORD.*
> *"For as the heavens are higher than the earth,*
> *So are My ways higher than your ways*
> *And My thoughts than your thoughts.*
> *"For as the rain and the snow come down from heaven,*
> *And do not return there without watering the earth*

And making it bear and sprout,
And furnishing seed to the sower and bread to the eater;
So will My word be which goes forth from My mouth;
It will not return to Me empty,
Without accomplishing what I desire,
And without succeeding in the matter for which I sent it.
"For you will go out with joy
And be led forth with peace;
The mountains and the hills will break forth into shouts of joy
before you,
And all the trees of the field will clap their hands.
"Instead of the thorn bush the cypress will come up,
And instead of the nettle the myrtle will come up,
And it will be a memorial to the LORD,

For an everlasting sign which will not be cut off."
(Isaiah 55:6–13 NASB)

I've never met an Appalachian who does not know the stabbing of a thorn bush's briars or hasn't at one time or another been stung by a nettle's stinging hairs. Because in this world there is both good and bad among us; blackberry picking always results in blood before the bushelful of fruit returns. While scars may remain, all bleeding stops eventually. I'm not sure God will require us to climb a cypress or a myrtle, a weeping willow or a maple prior to His return. God is just but He isn't callous. God wants us to keep looking for growing saplings while we are bleeding and stinging from briars and nettles.

When the too young are dyin', preachers are charged to offer this reconciling compress.

CHAPTER IV

WILL YOU SHOW ME
TO THE DOOR?

"Death is a door, and falling is just learning to stand."
Redwoods and Daises, Jason Upton

L osing a loved one, truth be told, is probably more akin to the little
brother who is not allowed to come along with his older brother to
the most wonderful of parties than it is to have his older brother move
from home never to return, be seen, nor heard from again. Some have
already received their invitations. Some have not, and many of those
who have not believe themselves not only to be left out but stolen from.
Sadly, the tendency of too many is to view death as finality rather than
as an adventure. Certainly, the pain and tragedy of death is to be served
with compassion. Yet when we view death only as an erasure rather than
fulfillment for the purpose of perfect intimacy, we hurt the heart of God.
God wants to be with us with nothing coming between us, but when death
arrives for others we defer to loneliness rather than solitude. We witness
the agony of death and hate the physical pain and deterioration that so
often accompanies it. Because the physicality of eternity is improbable
to see, the uncertainty of what is to come results in anxiety. Worse yet,

many cover their eyes from death like a child who fearfully cries, "It's not there! It's not there! It's not there!" Death is still very much alive, but death can die. God desires for us to know life here so we will know life there. This life is just simply a waiting of the turn until it is our turn, and our waiting our turn is to be filled with hopefulness.

What follows are three stories of hope. The first is the account of a very old woman named Fern who was one of the woodwork members of my childhood church. The second is that of a proper lady who was also a coal miner's wife. Her name is Loretta. The third is the testimony of a man named Nate who was born into the family of God hardly knowing he was living his last days on earth. In the testaments of these three, there is a calling to tell others the truth of the other side; there is an offering of hope that declares the child of God will know her way to the everlasting passageway when the time comes; and there is the promise that life becomes even more timeless as we grow peace with death's door.

†

Fern Martin knew me long before I knew her. She and her mother, Ma Crockett, rented my parents their first apartment just as soon as the two got married. They were there for the birth of my sister, Keely, and they were there for the changing of my first diapers, too. While I do not recall Ma's face as ever-present at our little United Methodist Church as Fern's, Ma was certainly Christian. Yet it was Fern I always remember sitting on her cushion on the back pew, left side of the pew looking forward, right side of the sanctuary looking forward—preachers looking out towards the congregation invert their rights and lefts.

Everyone in Appalachian churches knows whose seat is whose, but that's another story and another lesson.

Fern was one of those women who always seemed old. She was short, but not too short. She was thin but not sickly. Her hair was always a blue-gray and done without fail every Saturday morning so as to be ready for church on Sunday. Her skin was wrinkled, but her wrinkles were stately. I don't remember her wearing makeup, but she always smelled like drugstore perfume. She was frail but strong. There was never a time when I did not want to hug Fern, but I was certain that if I squeezed her a little too hard, even with my little boy strength, I just might break her. Still, Fern was the perfect example of the Proverbs 31 woman who is described in this way:

> *"Strength and dignity are her clothing, and she smiles at the future. She opens her mouth in wisdom, and the teaching of kindness is on her tongue. She looks well to the ways of her household, and does not eat the bread of idleness. Her children rise up and bless her; her husband also, and he praises her, saying: 'Many daughters have done nobly, but you excel them all.' Charm is deceitful and beauty is vain, but a woman who fears the Lord, she shall be praised. Give her the product of her hands, and let her works praise her in the gates."*
>
> *(Proverbs 31:25–31 NASB)*

I loved and still love Fern very much.

I do not remember when Fern died or how Fern died, but I do remember the lesson she offered before she walked from this world into the next. She did not pull me to the side and tell me this story alone, nor did she stand and offer testimony during our standard time of joys and concerns within the Sunday order of worship. Regardless of when this tale was told, Fern assured us that the journey beyond death to life is not as far a distance as one would think.

Fern was sleeping one night and had a dream. She dreamt that she was standing in the most beautiful field imaginable, that is except for the field that stood on the other side of the most beautiful river ever imaginable. Fern was blessed by the side of the river in which she found herself, but within her there was an unselfish and almost perfectly humble desire to get to the field on the other side. The river was too swift and too wide to cross, so Fern walked the riverbank until she came to a perfectly constructed and more than sturdy wooden bridge that spanned the river and connected the two fields of noncompeting beauty.

Fern took her first step onto the bridge, then her second, and then another and another. She was excited but certainly not anxious. She held within her a sense of the most appropriate anticipation.

And there He was. It was Jesus of Nazareth standing in the middle of the bridge.

Fragile Fern's legs could not carry her fast enough to the Savior, though she put them to good use. Each length she ran, Fern's legs grew stronger and stronger. She was being renewed with the running.

When she reached Jesus she wasn't out of breath but full of breath, and Fern said, "Oh, Lord, how I have waited for this moment."

Jesus simply smiled and let her hold Him.

As Fern loosened her embrace, she expected Jesus to now hold her and walk this little sister of His to the other more beautiful side.

But Jesus did not. The Messiah held Fern at arm's length and would not allow her to take any additional steps. Jesus looked into Fern's questioning eyes and said, "You cannot come with Me yet, Fern. It isn't your time."

Fern turned back into the old woman, no longer the young lady, and said, "No, Lord. I have given my life to You. I have lived for You and I have served You. Please, please, Lord, you cannot make me go back. I won't have it."

With lionlike eyes, Jesus looked at Fern and said, "You must. You must go back and tell people what you have seen here. You will be with us soon enough."

Fern attempted one more, "Please," but it failed to move past her heart and over her lips. She knew her Savior was right. She had to go back and tell.

Fern woke in tears, but knew she had been called to tell.

Fern would be with them soon.

As instructed, Fern told us.

Soon Fern was permitted to cross the bridge, and those of us to whom she told the story have been sharing the hope of the other side since. It is why Fern saw. It is why Fern told. It is why we continue to tell.

We have to tell the story so that people have hope of everlasting life.

✝

Loretta Chase's home sat adjacent to a street named Sunset. Before I knew her, when I was just a boy, her yard was the battlefield for one of my childhood fistfights. No one should ever get in a fistfight in someone else's yard, especially when that yard touches a street named Sunset.

Well, many years later, the fistfights had ended, I had grown up, and started an Evangelical Methodist Church in the same town where I had been born, bred, and raised. I knew one of Loretta's daughters, Loretta's son-in-law, and grandkids very well, so when Kingdom Evangelical Methodist Church began the first Sunday of December 1998, a lot of well-wishers from my hometown soon followed, including Loretta and this portion of her family. Loretta ended up being far more than a well-wisher. If I remember correctly, Loretta started attending Kingdom on the third or fourth Sunday, and after that, Loretta rarely missed a Sunday. I was far closer to her daughter and daughter's family, but it was Loretta who first committed to the family of Kingdom.

Now, I was raised by a Marine father who owned a machine shop and a school teacher mother, so I was expected to keep my hair short, my shirt tucked in, and be ever certain to make my bed and cut grass with perfectly straight lines. Yet I still possessed the heart of a poet. The older I became, the more the poet came out. And while in the early days of Kingdom there was still a fair share of Hell's fire and brimstone, let's just say I was becoming more free in my ministry.

My freedom in Christ afforded me the opportunity to preach away from a pulpit, occasionally in blue jeans, and with many vivid illustrations. This was more than fine for me and people like me, but Appalachia is a place of old mountains. Elders prefer the stability of a pulpit, a suit and tie, and illustrations of a more black and white variety. Suffice to say, while Loretta was always among Kingdom's most faithful parishioners, she did not always approve of my ... *foolishness*.

I loved Loretta, though.

And Loretta loved me.

There were just some things I continued to do, and there were just some things Loretta critiqued. Between us, it was as much a professional relationship as it was personal. While only once or twice Loretta and I found ourselves in a heated disagreement, the bond between us was far stronger than any discord experienced. Our friendship went on like that for years.

In 2006, Loretta's husband died a couple weeks after the Fourth of July and, within seven years, right before Christmas, Loretta was getting ready to follow him. I'm relatively sure it was a Friday afternoon I went to see Loretta. I drove the short drive from the church to her home nestled next to Sunset. I walked up to the porch, knocked quietly on the sliding glass door, and let myself in. It was just the nurse and Loretta in that side room where I had spent so many afternoons with Loretta. This time, though, Loretta wasn't sitting in her chair. This time, Loretta was alive but unconscious and lying in her hospital bed.

I took a seat and began small-talking with the nurse. There were base-level pleasantries, and then I asked the standard ministerial questions, like, "Has she been resting comfortably? What is the last time she ate or drank? Have the hospice nurses given you any indication as to when?" I was there for about thirty minutes asking questions such as those. Loretta never moved, and while I know the unconscious hear far more than we give them the ability to hear, this time the sounds Loretta was primarily hearing, I was certain, were those from another land.

I looked at the nurse and said, "Well, I'm going to go. Would you like to pray with me before I leave?" The nurse did not even have time to answer. Loretta sat straight up in bed, as conscious as I had even seen before. I said, "Well, hello there, Loretta." She returned the hello.

With the nurse sitting quietly and politely looking on, Loretta and I had our final conversation together. It is a rare thing in life to get to say everything that needs to be said to someone before death comes, yet Loretta and I did just that. There's really no need to tell you what we spoke about. As kindly as I can say this, it's really none of your business. Trust me, though, Loretta and I said everything that needed said. There were apologies, and we said "Thank you" and "I love you" to one another. Then I asked Loretta if she would like to pray. She agreed.

We prayed, and when the "Amen" was offered, Loretta opened her eyes to me one last time and said something to me, peculiar but familiar.

Loretta asked me, "Will you show me to the door?"

I smiled and said, "Loretta, you know your way to the door. You don't need me to show you."

Loretta smiled at me, nodded her head, and whether I said it or she said it, it does not matter except that the words were said: "I'll see you on the other side."

I left through the sliding glass door.

Loretta soon left through the everlasting door.

We all need hope to know that the child of God knows her way when the time comes. She just needs to trust what she has learned and lived believing.

✝

There was once a stately Korean woman who began attending Kingdom. She did so alone. She was Christian. Her husband was not. But she wanted him to be. We became friends and began to pray for her husband, Nate. Not long after, Nate also began attending Sunday services.

Now, there are some in this world who deny the existence of God altogether. Some others aren't quite sure whether there is a God or not. Some are convinced God exists, and they believe if their good done in life outweighs their bad done in life, then all will be well when they get to the other side.

Then there are those who believe there is a necessity for a Messiah. It is a simple theology, but simple is never simpler. They believe:

God is holy. Humanity is not. Humanity's unholiness separates us from Him, and the gap between the two sides is too great a chasm to bridge. Jesus of Nazareth was born of a virgin, fully God and fully man. He lived life without sin and allowed Himself to die on a cross. When He died, He found Himself on the side which humanity stands. Yet, because He did not sin, He never had to let go of the side of holiness and the presence of God. The chasm between death and life has been bridged through Jesus Christ. He died. He was buried. He rose again from the dead. People then have to decide whether or not this makes sense intellectually, and when it does, then they have to stand and live their lives submitted to this ideology.

That is the most basic definition of what it means to give one's life to Christ.

This is what my Korean friend wanted for her American-born husband.

Nate was still deciding.

She hoped but never pushed. I preached but never demanded. Nate had the space he needed to decide on his own.

Now, some would say that when Nate found out he had brain cancer, he decided to give his life to Christ out of fear. I do not disagree. When Nate found out he had an inoperable brain tumor, he decided he needed to make the decision. People come to the Lord for one of two reasons: either they are inspired or desperate. While every preacher prefers a road of inspiration, we are neither naive to nor ashamed of the fact that most come to salvation by way of desperation. Nate was desperate, and he came to Christ.

Nate kept attending church, kept receiving radiation and chemotherapy treatments, but nothing was helping. Nate had come to his final days. Nate had been raised in the church, baptized as a baby, grew up and went through all of Christianity's rites of passage. Yet, this time Jesus was the

Savior of the grown man's choosing. Nate called me and asked if we could baptize him somewhere.

We had no baptismal, but my friend's father was an apostolic minister on the other side of town. They had a baptismal and were willing to share, so Nate and I headed over to the church by ourselves one Sunday afternoon. It was winter, and that water was freezing cold. There Nate and I were struggling to get him down into that baptismal. We made it in, though, and holding my friend in my arms, I asked him, "Nate, do you believe in Jesus Christ as your Lord and Savior?"

Nate said, "Yes."

I then put him under that cold water and said, "Nate, I baptize you in the name of the Father, the Son, and the Holy Spirit." I lifted Nate from the water, we embraced, and my friend was now anointed as my brother.

In this world, our brotherhood only lasted a few more months. I was called by Nate's wife, and she said we were now very close. I headed straight to their house. Nate's wife said she would give the two of us some time alone together. What followed has remained one of the most spiritually transformational conversations of my life.

Nate and I were openly talking about his death when he looked at me and shared this simple truth, saying, "You know, Kevin... as soon as my mother got there, I'll be there... and as soon as I get there, you'll be there too."

I had never discerned everlasting life like that before. Certainly, I knew the apostle John's revelatory reporting that declares:

"And the city has no need of the sun or of the moon to shine on it, for the glory of God has illumined it, and its lamp is the Lamb. The nations will walk by its light, and the kings of the earth will bring their glory into it. In the daytime (for there will be no night there) its gates will never be closed; and they will bring the glory and the honor of the nations into it; and nothing unclean, and no one who practices abomination and lying, shall

ever come into it, but only those whose names are written in the Lamb's book of life."

(REVELATION 21:23–27 NASB)

Yet, until Nate had laid it so cleanly before me, I had given this truth no consideration.

Nate passed days later.

Now I know. While the living are confined by time and space here, those who have passed on are neither confined nor waiting. This truth goes against a great many of the hymns nestled in the old, brown, Cokesbury Hymnal that wrongly reminds us our loved ones are *waiting* for us on the other side. Our loved ones aren't waiting; they are living, turning, and seeing us there. When we acknowledge this truth, the more clearly we can see the door. The more clearly we see the door, the more timeless life both here and there becomes.

✝

So death is a door and we must live our lives pointing people to the peace of the gateway. Death's door is not one that is hidden or void of an exit sign. When we have lived life as children of God, we can trust we will know our way to the entrance when the time comes. And yet, the greatest beauty is in the truth that death can die. The finality of death dies when we see within our expiring existence the timelessness of life. It is a timelessness that doesn't have to be waited upon or avoided. It is a timelessness that can begin today.

Comfort one another with these words.

CHAPTER V

DEATH'S PILGRIMAGE

The doctor stood over him. For weeks he had been unresponsive, so this will be the final cry for hope. The doctor was tall and thick, and that body of his housed a booming voice. The hulking MD simply hovered over the twenty-something-year-old man and shouted his name.

"Robbie!"

We held our breath as the doctor gathered his next one.

"Robbie!"

There was no response. There was no twitch. There was no blink. There was nothing. There was simply a machine to keep his lungs inhaling and exhaling, and another machine causing his heart to beat. Robbie was gone.

The place where we had holed up for nearly two months had to be emptied out, so that the next family could come in and begin their prayers for signs of life.

Our hope for signs was over.

It was time to leave the hospital and begin death's pilgrimage.

With every death comes a journey, a crusade, a mission. It begins as family and friends leave the deathbed. This is the first step, and be assured if loved ones are to reach the destination that reconciles loss with all the coming tomorrows, then many other steps will follow. Where there has been the gain of birth, then the loss of death will be its appropriate counterpart. Birth's unwelcome, complimentary conclusion cannot be avoided any more than it should be celebrated. Only a fool praises a goodbye that has no return. Yet, death's pilgrimage knows that while the one gone will not return, the remaining pilgrims can journey to tomorrow's new normalcy and the healing that ultimately reunites them to the one gone away.

And so they travel on.

There is another grieving mother, and he is her thirty-eight-year-old baby, manslaughtered. On her left she is held up by her equally grieving but strong-for-her husband. To her right is her daughter-in-law and her granddaughter. The funeral directors and I are following behind.

She does not float, but her legs certainly are neither supporting nor carrying her. The closer to the casket, the greater her collapse. Behind her, we ready a chair. In the twenty feet we walk towards the coffin, into that chair she falls twenty times. It is a backbreaking pilgrimage to the casket's first offering.

She made it.

They all made it.

A crumbling mother falls at her daughter's coffin. This time a gun hasn't taken the child's life. This time it is a hypodermic needle emptied of its fentanyl-laced heroin. Though we stand beside her, she kneels alone, nearly sitting, to pray. Her words are the fulfillment of Paul's prophecy that says:

"In the same way the Spirit also helps our weakness; for we do not know how to pray as we should, but the Spirit Himself intercedes for us with groaning too deep for words; and He who searches the hearts knows what the mind of the Spirit is, because He intercedes for the saints according to the will of God."

(ROMANS 8:26, 27 NASB)

He strengthens her, and she rises to her feet as they see their daughter for the first time like this and never again as they think back to all the times before.

Most of the time it is younger looking in at older. Some of the time it is older looking in at younger. It is grandchildren looking in at Grandma. It is children looking in at Dad. It is best friend looking in at old friend. Most likely, it is wife looking in at husband. Less likely, it is husband looking in at wife.

After the flowers have arrived and been positioned, but before those who will pay their respects come, there is an initial looking in at the body lying in the casket. The clothes are right. The hair is right. Tears stream, some steadily, some slowly, all heartfelt.

"He looks good," she says.

"She looks like she's sleeping," he says.

"He had been so sick. He'd just lost so much weight. You did a good job though," they say.

Tears are wiped. Hugs are given. Those closest to the one gone now begin to mill about the room looking at old pictures and noting who is thoughtful enough to send flowers. This is the first looking-in, but a long night of looking-in awaits.

The doors open. The people begin to line up and sign the register book. The family is assembled casket-side and begin looking in, looking in, and looking in again. From 3:00 to 5:00, and from 7:00 to 9:00 they look in, look in, and look in again until they want to look in no more.

The night is over.

They exhale and prepare to go home.

One last look in.

Tomorrow they will not want to look away from the sight they will always be tempted to remember.

Morning comes and there is light once again. The sun may appear, or it may hide itself behind the clouds. Maybe there's a chill in the air and the vibrancy of autumn. Perhaps it is snowing. The tulips may be taking their first spring breaths. Are there thunderstorms? Regardless of the weather, tomorrow is now today, and with today come the most wearying steps of the pilgrimage.

The previous night was more of a reunion than an evening of visitation. Today is different. The pall that will eventually cover the casket is not the only pall in the room. There is a pall that calls them to wonder, *Will I ever see him again?*

Soon the preacher walks in, pauses at the casket, and everyone goes silent. He strides the three steps to the pulpit's perch and says with somber tones, "Will you bow with me in an opening word of prayer?"

The back row cries far less than the front row, but all are appropriate as the Scriptures are read, the songs play, and the eulogy is offered. In his mind, the preacher questions, *Do they hear any hope or reconciliation at all?* He offers his closing prayer, and soon person upon person is looking in and filing past, paying their last respects. Even those who do not typically kiss and hug surrender to the comforting acts of intimacy.

Each of them, in their own way, says to those who remain:

"It's been far too long."

"I love you."

"We will have to get together soon in a happier place than here."

The front row nods in approval, but somehow all know this will be the last time until the next time.

Soon, all that are left can be found in the front row.

The grandchildren look in first.

The children look in second.

Finally, the wife who almost made it to fifty years of marriage with him is the last to look in.

The preacher is standing to the side, respectfully waiting. And after the looking in has been long enough, the funeral director almost in a whisper says, "What stays?"

Is he to be buried with the pictures? Is she to be buried with the poem? Is the wedding band and engagement ring to be left, or will they both be removed so dying people can fight over the dying things once belonging to the now dead? The wife, the husband, the father, the mother, the eldest child gives his orders, they all collect their things and head from the chapel so the funeral directors can prepare the casket holding his body for transport to the final resting place.

They linger out.

One man cannot bring himself to walk away.

Sixteen years ago, the man's son went to the hospital emergency room for a migraine. The hospital staff could not ease his pain. Soon the migraine being suffered from in the ER mutated into a coma that drove the young man to the intensive care unit. For two months the man held vigil over his son.

Now, the man looks into *this casket* and remembers the doctor standing over *his son*. Now, the man looks into *this casket* and remembers that final cry for hope. The man remembers the tall, thick doctor with the booming voice. Now, he remembers the hulking MD standing over his twenty-something-year-old son and how he shouted *his son's name*. Looking into *this casket*, the sixteen-year-old echoes of *his son's* name once again haunt him.

"Robbie!"

Remembering then and looking in now, the man has no breath left.

"Robbie!"

The man looks in now and remembers then: There was no response. There was no twitch. There was no blink. There was nothing. There was only a machine keeping his lungs inhaling and exhaling, and another machine causing *his son's* heart to beat.

Robbie was gone.

And now this man, who sixteen years prior looked into the casket of his son, stands alone looking into the casket of his grandson, Ethan.

What had grown stale is now fresh.

Different has given birth to new.

It is a journey the man never thought he would have to take again.

That time, and this time... both times, he has done so with brokenness and courage.

There are processions that stretch for miles, and there are processions made up of a hearse and one car. Once there was a funeral procession for a young motocross racer. Harleys and Hondas led the procession. The rumbling of their engines generated so much force the funeral coach was shaking. Still, no matter the amount of vehicles, the presence of the procession is no less silent within the speeding-by and less-than-concerned world. Paid attention to or ignored, every funeral procession makes its presence known as it paints its trail of death through city streets; and, in the death-dyed lanes, to those who today are not a part of the procession, Wisdom cries to them, saying, "One day you will be."

The cemetery welcomes another procession. There is a tent, six feet of dirt piled and covered beside a soon-to-be-refilled hole, and the cap of the vault. No one ever notices these things. The gazes of those who mourn are elsewhere and nowhere. The tent, dirt, hole, and the vault cap are never offended. The business of burial is politely detached. These things just silently and without emotion wait their turn.

While the final cars are being parked, the pallbearers proceed to the back of the funeral coach, the casket is removed, and the preacher leads the way to the graveside where he will stand at the casket's head.

It is raining now.

They huddle together in their black, sunglasses, and umbrellas as they hold tattered tissues and one another.

These are not those who read the obituary in the newspaper and never came to pay their respects. Nor are they the ones who came to the visitation and said, "I'm so sorry for your loss." They also are not the others who attended both the visitation and the funeral, but when asked by the funeral directors if they would be going to the cemetery, they said, "No. I have to get back to work." These are the ones who find themselves in the cemetery's valley and are praying that God is with them rather than what appears to be only death's shadows. From individual frames of reference, each has been walking for three or more days from the deathbed to the graveside. Very soon the last steps of death's pilgrimage will be taken.

Spouses sit. Children sit. Elderly relatives who have been here most before sit. The pallbearers stand behind them to steady their chairs. The funeral director nods. The preacher reads from the Psalms, speaks of the body's return to the ground; he offers Revelation's hope of no more tears, then one final prayer and a benediction.

Finality's finish line has now arrived and with it the calling to take one last step.

The funeral director says, "This concludes our services. You may now return to your cars."

There may or may not be a luncheon provided at a church fellowship hall. Right now, that is the last thing on the minds of the widow, the son, the granddaughter, the parent, the best friend. Each of these have walked from the deathbed, to the initial sight, to the visitation, to the tomorrow now today, to the funeral, to the last look in before the closing of the casket, to the processional, to the funeral procession, to the service of committal. Now, they've been given permission to walk away.

How far a walk is it from a casket suspended above a grave to a waiting car and a life of very different normalcy?

For those still placing single roses on the casket, the most intense questioning begins. How does a person walk all these steps and then simply return to his car, drive back to the church, eat a meal, and then turn the key of life's ignition?

It cannot be that easy.

Such is the reason so many just sit and stare at the casket. Certainly, after the leaving there will be a return with flowers to the site on his birthday, their anniversary, Memorial Day, the Fourth of July, Christmas, and the day of her death, but those days will be very different from this day. This day the flowers are still in bloom, the casket is polished and in view, loving hands still rest upon it, and all those who heeded the funeral director's release and returned to their cars cannot leave yet, because the cars of those who still weep are at the front of the procession empty and parked. They tell themselves if the moment can be maintained, life will remain as it has always been.

Sadly, it will never be as it has been.

At some point, death's pilgrimage is complete when you allow yourself to walk away.

Then ... a pilgrimage of absence.

The antidote for grief is not a stiff upper lip, nor the holding back of tears, nor masquerading laughter, nor anger, nor avoidance. Grief's antidote is vulnerability.

As a body lies lifeless on its deathbed, to give oneself permission to lose one's breath and to unlock the choking down of the throat's lump requires the courage of vulnerability.

Then with vulnerability a single step is taken.

To walk into the funeral home, go through the chapel's doors, approach the casket, no matter how long it takes, no matter how far you fall, then to cry out, "Why?" and then rise to look into the casket first, requires the courage of vulnerability.

Then with vulnerability the second step is taken.

As old friends, new friends, best friends, and people you never expected to be there come in and require you to look in, look in, and look in again, the courage of vulnerability is required.

Then with vulnerability the third step is taken.

You wake up without the one beside you, the bed is cold, and you can still smell her in the fibers of the sheets you haven't yet changed, but light still pours in your window. You get dressed and you go. You sit in the front row. You consider the messages present in the music, the poems, the prayers, and the Scriptures. You cry when you recall the things you will miss the most. You laugh as you consider all the silly reasons you love her. You receive the preacher's "Amen." To be blessed by the funeral requires the courage of vulnerability.

A fourth step is taken, once again with vulnerability.

To look in one last time, walk away, and hear the casket close requires the courage of vulnerability.

Vulnerability carries the fifth step.

Ashes to ashes.

You know the rest, and while the rest provides no rest, you lay a rose on the casket and then your hand. One last kiss on the bronze that encompasses her. And you walk away with the courage of vulnerability that cries, saying, "She is not here. She is risen."

Content with your vulnerability, the sixth step has been taken.

Certainly grief's pain provides no Sabbath rest, but the honesty with which death's pilgrimage is taken reconciles who is gone with the one who is now here. Most certainly they will not return to us, but with each step taken we will one day find ourselves with them.

CHAPTER VI

SOMETHING TO CRY ABOUT

"But we do not want you to be uninformed, brethren, about those who are asleep, so that you will not grieve as do the rest who have no hope."

(1 THESSALONIANS 4:13 NASB)

I did not grow up in a coal town. I grew up in a small town. There were a few of us whose parents were public school teachers, or small business owners, and there was one of us whose dad was everyone's dentist; but, for the most part, all our moms stayed home and our dads left long before the sun rose or as it prepared to fall over the horizon to work all day or all night in the coal industry of West Virginia's hills.

Growing up, fighting was both permitted and expected ... crying was not. At one time or another—and some of us on a daily basis—all of us were warned by parents and principals who assured us with words of negative reinforcement, saying, "You stop that crying or I'll give you something to cry about." We never questioned those words. While I never heard of any of us speak of abuse, and none of us felt the need to report the swinging of the belt, all of us accepted those words that within us generated one kind of durability but failed to birth within us the bravery most needed.

I was ten years old when I first saw a man cry. It was October of 1980 and we were in the same funeral home I find myself in time and again today as a preacher of funerals. That day, I wasn't the one offering the eulogy. That day, I was just a boy and sitting a row behind my uncle Dave at my papaw's funeral. John Camp had been hard on his son, David Camp. So between how all of us had been raised for generations to be and the pain of my uncle's upbringing, I held no expectation for tears. I did as I had always been told and choked down my throat's lump, but my uncle Dave just let loose and began crying so hard. Now, even after thirty-eight years have passed, I can still remember how hard he was shaking. Until now, I have never spoken of it. I've just always wondered.

When my grandpap died, once again we were in the same funeral home. I remember my aunt Carol sitting next to me and holding my hand. On the day of Grandpap's funeral, his brother, my uncle Bob, who owned an auto body shop and was always the life of the party, couldn't gather the strength to come in the funeral home for his brother's funeral. Outside, he simply cried on the sidewalk. I did not cry. As a dutiful son I didn't think I was allowed, though I wanted to.

There are plenty of reasons to cry.

Sometimes people are not prepared for a person's passing. Other times, one half of you has died. Maybe it is a tragedy. Maybe he was just a child. There is physical and emotional pain. Within society and the heart, there is a void now present. We cry for what could have been and what should have been. We are uncertain. Could it be torment? Or is it rest?

Children cry as a way to communicate distress, and the apostle Paul teaches in his words to the Church at Rome that the rocks, hills, trees, and all creation groans with cries for Christ's return.

Is it ever appropriate to cry?

It is.

Tears are not reflections of weakness. Tears are a divine gift of grace that are to be a balm for our grieving souls. Certainly tears can be over-used as shackles that hinder the grieving from moving on; or tears are misused as a tool for gaining an advantage, but the value of tears shed far outweighs their side effects.

After an era of holding one's breath in uncertain agony, tears are the great exhale.

As children, there are always one or two among the passel of youths who seem to rise above and assume the role of leader. In leading, each becomes a hero. These heroes aren't only champions for their own generation, but also for the little kids not so far behind them. Then, as children transition to manhood, it seems like the true heroes never lose their heroic luster.

I was one of the little kids who looked up to one such hero.

As we became young men, the hero died.

I was called upon to bury him.

Hundreds of people were there that day. Every seat in our little sanctuary was filled and people were standing all along the walls. The fire marshal was not in attendance but if he were, he would not have approved.

We didn't care.

We had come to pay our respects to this fallen thirty-something-year-old champion.

As the prayers were prayed, the scriptures were read, the songs played, and the eulogy offered, there in front of a whole bunch of other boys-now-men who had been taught not to cry, the tears began to pour from my eyes. Thirty years of backed-up came gushing forth.

It took an hour-and-a-half to process the people past the casket that day. As I watched all those men who I used to battle on the little league fields pass the casket, they too were all crying.

We didn't have to stop our crying.

On that day, we had something to cry about.

Now I know no one needs to apologize for crying. Strength is not found in holding back tears. Strength is found in letting them all go. Yes sometimes we try to produce tears where they never should be, but when genuine grief is present it is quite appropriate to cry.

So, cry away. We are those who grieve with hope.

TALES OF RECONCILIATION

CHAPTER I

GET TO YOUR ALTAR

I s it possible to welcome the reconciliation Christ affords when you find your widowed mother lying in her kitchen murdered by her second husband, and then you are denied the chance of retributive confrontation as you immediately discover the man you may or may not have thought to be your stepfather, now a murderer, dead in the back bedroom from a self-inflicted gunshot wound? Virtually all choose to walk with the Christ as a result of inspiration or desperation, but a murder/suicide is neither. For the one who makes the gruesome finding, cries of vengeance and not salvific need appear to be the most logical of reactions.

The sun had not yet set on that early summer evening. It was still muggy, and there was uncertainty as to whether or not the cool of nightfall would be granted a place with the close of the day. Summer's mosquitos and humidity add to confrontational tension. Now required to be outside by law enforcement, the son and the daughter-in-law who had walked into the kitchen of the innocent murdered and then ran into the bedroom of the guilty murderer stood holding one another, still raining tears, still in deep shock. All those who lived next door were looking on, either well-intentioned up close or well-intentioned from their good-neighbor-making fences. The home, now house of horror, sat beside a busy neighborhood road, and, as car after car went past, the speed limit lowered as the need to look continued to rise. One by one family members of the murdered and the murderer began to arrive. While no active hostile exchanges occurred, both sides kept to their respective sides of their respective mother's and their respective father's property. This went on late into the night.

The sun was gone.

Stars shone upon the ground's darkness.

Much milling, but no movement was about.

The middle-aged son who had found his mother was a relatively new parishioner. His wife was my oldest son's kindergarten teacher, and he was a bailiff for a local circuit court judge. I knew of him. He knew of me. They had begun attending my local assembly as a result of a funeral he had attended that I had officiated.

The service was for a well-known local bar owner turned Christian. I knew the beer garden proprietor quite well on both sides of his reception of Christ's extension of reconciliation, so during the eulogy, some of the stories brought great laughter to the somber day (I had reported to my mother, after the funeral, that the laughter was so raucous at times during the funeral I believed we were bordering on sacrilege).

With his wife as my son's teacher, our knowledge of one another, and then the prodigal-come-home's hilariously, near-the-edge funeral, the bailiff and the kindergarten teacher made the decision to make our church their household's regular spiritual stomping grounds. Yet, it was not until this deathly night did we bring together a needing and offering intimacy of Christ's compassionate and raw-honesty-welcoming love.

My most recent sermon series had asked: *Just exactly what is an altar?* Certainly, every Appalachian who had ever sung from the brown Cokesbury Hymnal and who had received their granny's death grip on their leg for squirming during church knows what an altar is. The altar is the place where to which the sometimes sweaty but always impassioned preacher bids his convicted but mostly condemned congregation to run at the end of his Hell's fire and brimstone sermon… *or at least that was what we all had been taught*. Those who went forward to the three feet-tall kneeler—sometimes with spindles, sometimes with wood paneling, but always with a top rail for confessional prayer—were the ones in the greatest immediate or overall spiritual distress. While no one ever would own up to it, nearly everyone whispered in hushed tones as to the specifics of each sinful pilgrim who in tears headed towards the front of the sanctuary as the choir began to sing, *"Amazing grace, how sweet the sound that saved a wretch like me!"* The sanctuary's altar alone, in the sanctuary where running was strictly prohibited, was the one place to which to run to get saved.

That was the mantra.

With full disclosure, under that mantra and at such an altar, at the ripe age of ten I had genuinely welcomed the reconciliation of Jesus. But after many years of spiritual abuse inflicted by compassionless, legalist preachers dedicated to keeping people in their local churches and denominations rather than the bosom of the Lord, something had to give. Certainly folks need to be made aware of the chasm present in humanity's spiritual condition for which death, burial, and resurrection of Messiah became and remains good news. Yet the opportunity to faithfully kneel while crying at the feet of Christ and receive His restorative and reconciling touch is not to be confined simply to the little brown church in the vale. God's words to all of us during that season of preaching said, "Get to *your altar.*" If *your altar* is a church sanctuary altar, then run on up there. If *your altar* is a pile of laundry at the foot of your teenager's bed, then find yourself on the floor. If *your altar* is a bathmat at the base of your commode, then fall on your knees in the place of your home which has welcomed the greatest nakedness.

Sunday upon Sunday that bailiff, that husband of the kindergarten teacher, that son, that discoverer-of-his-murdered-mother had been listening to these inclusive words of the exclusive Christ's offer of reconciliation. So there in the midst of death, tension, police tape, and tears, that man took me by the arm and, spying his twin brother's front porch stoop next door to their mother's home, that broken man said to me, "You've been saying for weeks, 'Get to *your altar.*' My brother's front porch stoop is as good an altar as any. In the middle of all this bad, will you kneel with me and pray to welcome into my life Jesus' Good News?"

Together we ran to his altar.

Just like that sinful woman at Simon's house who Simon refused to look at but Jesus never took His eyes off of...

Just like that man on the mat whose sins were forgiven by Jesus because of the faith of his four ceiling-demolishing friends...

Just like that confessing criminal who walked into paradise with the King...

Just like the centurion bathed in Jesus' blood and body fluids who declared, "Truly this man is the Son of God...."

There, where it seems like cries of vengeance and not salvific need appear to be the most logical of reactions, a broken man knelt upon some boards of pressure-treated wood and said, "Jesus, have mercy on me."

In that night of such darkness, instead of death, destruction, and thievery there was life, and life more abundant.

CHAPTER II

GOTTA SUDS UP

Bill Chase was a nice, old coal miner who I buried a number of years ago.

He was short, sort of gray, sort of bald, and had big ears and a big nose like so many old men are required to have sculpted on their heads as their last days begin to take hold. Bill reminded me of the cartoon characterization of Jimmy Durante from the Christmas television cartoon, *Frosty the Snowman*. His parents were immigrants, and Bill was from Westover, West Virginia. Some say nothing good can come from either.

Like so many others who get the short end of the prejudicial stick, Bill brought much good.

The story of his reception of Jesus' gift of reconciliation hearkens to two well-known Bible passages: *the feeding of the 5000 and the Rich Young Ruler*. Now for Bill his testimony lines up with the day after Jesus multiplies the poor boy's lunch of five barley loaves and two fish, and since I'm sharing stories of reconciliation, Bill's response to the Good Master's offer was contrary to that of the Rich Young Ruler. Bill walks with God, and he does so because he minded Jesus' words to labor for that which will never perish and because he chose to rise from the mine of death's darkness when Jesus offered him the vibrancy of light and life.

Many Appalachian men do not prioritize going to church on Sunday morning. Yes, they believe in God. If they didn't, how else does a man have the courage to descend thousands of feet through a coal mining shaft into the darkness where a headlamp and a few roof bolts is all that rests between the miner and thousands of tons of certain death? So Bill, too, did not prioritize church; and Bill, too, like so many Appalachians, was the sole bread winner, so weekend and holiday time-and-a-half was money much needed to feed his wife and three daughters.

From his teens to his gray hair, Bill lived the life of a West Virginia coal miner. His wife, Loretta, would rise with him long before dawn, pack his bucket, give him a kiss, say, goodbye, and then until the end of his shift, Loretta would pray all day for his safe return. While coal dust can never be completely washed from a miner's pores, not a speck of coal dust was ever present in the Chase family home. Some minimize the beauty of keeping a clean house, but when a family has simple means and provision, and the patriarch and matriarch are products of the Great Depression, everything with which they have been blessed is cared for with stewardship that is mindful of God's provision.

Bill mined coal and provided for his wife and daughters.

Loretta prayed for Bill, kept a good home and good girls, and saw to it that four out of the five went to church Sunday after Sunday.

Quietly, during all those prayers for Bill's safety, Loretta prayed that one day her husband would allow the Suffering Servant to wash her husband's feet stained with dying coal dust.

I came into the picture long after Bill retired from the mines.

Loretta and two of her daughters—now with children and grandchildren of their own—began attending my church. Her other daughter married a preacher, and the preacher son-in-law and daughter-now-preacher's-wife pastored a church in Bucyrus, Ohio.

For many years, Loretta had prayed for Bill to be with her and their daughters at the end of each day. Now, with a well-intentioned and scripturally sound mindset, Loretta was concerned about Bill being with her for eternity. She asked me if I would be willing to make a visit to their home.

I did.

I did.

I did.

And I did.

I loved Loretta, her daughters, the grandchildren, every single one of them. I was getting to know Bill, and I loved him too. I was raised in my father's hydraulic machine shop—welding, machining, and getting in the way—but all those days in the machine shop and around coal mining gave Bill and me something to talk about before we ever started talking about Jesus. You see, coal mining was part of the reason Bill welcomed me, and he knew how much I loved—and still love—his family. But frankly, just like Jesus multiplied the five loaves and two fish in order to bring about an opportunity to call people to the Gospel, I also brought food into the equation so that Bill would be receptive to the message of Jesus' good news.

Any coal miner worth his metatarsal boots has some kind of snack cakes packed in his dinner bucket for mealtime in the dinner hole. For some it's Little Debbie Snack Cakes, and for others it's those oatmeal pies with the super sweet white icing sandwiched in between. Yet for Bill it was Hostess Snowballs, Twinkies, and Ho Hos. Those supermarket pastries were packed without fail in Bill's bucket, and every time I headed to the Chase's home I went with my version of five loaves and two fish: *Hostess snack cakes*. Some would call it bait and switch, or maybe even a bribe, but I figured if Jesus compassionately multiplied a little kid's food for the masses on one day in order to bring them back the next day so that He could share His Good News, then it was going to have to be my plan of attack too.

In the side television room of their home, I'd sit on the couch as Bill and Loretta were flanking one another in dueling La-Z-Boy recliners.

Bill and I would shoot the breeze for a while over a Twinkie or three.

I'd share with Bill the Good News of Jesus.

Loretta would pray silently to herself.

Then Bill would always say he just wasn't ready.

Bill began coming to Sunday services, and his belief in God never waned, but to allow Jesus to wash a life of coal dust from him, well, for whatever reason Bill was always hesitant. Bill never claimed it was a personal feeling of inferiority or unworthiness, but somehow, even without saying, you could see in his eyes his knowledge of the great chasm that separates every individual from the God Who desires marriage to each one. Bill never spoke negatively about any churches nor the preachers who played a role in the fostering of his wife's so strongly-established faith. His honesty only afforded words of edification and not words of destructive gossip. He valued the family of God without yet being part of it, and he longed for relationship but was not going to cheaply claim hereditary title.

During all my visits, Loretta's prayers, and the church services on Sunday, Bill was being proposed to by the Holy Spirit, saying, "You lack one thing: Sell everything you have, give to the poor, and come follow Me." Yet, as a humble traditionalist, Bill wrongly believed it was his responsibility to ask the Father for the bride's hand in marriage rather than the truth with which he was being faced, namely being the bride proposed to by the Bridegroom. For strong, honest, proud men who are accustomed to offering proposals as they believe a common gentleman should, it is more than difficult to receive one.

Jesus said to the Rich Young Ruler, "Why do you call Me good? Only God is good."

The fact that Bill Chase refused to claim godliness is the evidence for his goodness. For this miner of coal the diamond was now before him, and he knew he had not labored one second, with one drop of blood to extract it from its holy place.

It was just there.

With great simplicity the day's wage was being freely offered to him, and he could not justify it in his good self.

So I just kept going.

I loved Bill and I loved his friendship, and honestly I never saw Bill as a mark like so many self-serving evangelists see folks as they head out door-to-door to do some soul-winnin'. At Bill's funeral, just such a woman said to me, "What if he would have died while you were bringing him all those snack cakes?" I still choose not to answer such pious critics. My prayer is for those who will never understand that they will taste and see that the Lord is good.

With Hostess snack cakes under my arm and love in my heart, I visited the Chases again and again.

We have made the word *simple* something to be looked down upon, but I have come to learn that simple is never simpler. On an afternoon in 2003, a simple young man offered a simple old man a simple message for the thousandth time, and finally the simple old man received the proposal with great joy.

After all those visits, and with much knowledge of my old friend, I asked Bill a question, "Bill, how many years did you work in the mines?"

"Too many to mention," Bill answered.

With well-intentioned patronization I asked Bill, "Were you dirty with coal dust each day as you came up out of the mine?"

Patiently Bill played along and answered my second question, "Yes, Kevin. When I came up from underground I was covered from head-to-toe with coal dust."

I continued to press, saying, "Did they have a shower room at the mines?"

"Yes," Bill answered.

"Soap and water?" I questioned.

With patience growing dangerously thin, Bill answered, saying, "Yes."

"Just one more question," I said. "Could you believe with all your heart that the soap and water in the shower could get you clean, but never get in the shower and expect to go home clean as a whistle and have Loretta not yell at you for bringing coal dust into the house?"

Bill's simple response to my simple question walked us to the feet of the Lord. The old Appalachian miner simply answered, "No, Kevin. You'd have to get in the shower and suds up."

Nothing more needed to be said. The simple message of Christ's love for the good but yet-unwilling-to-follow man had emerged from the darkness of the mine. Bill certainly wasn't rich or young, and most of the time Loretta ruled the roost, but in that moment, after enough barley loaves and fish to feed five thousand, Bill Chase put out his coal-dusted feet and allowed the Host of the wedding feast to wash him.

Bill Chase had more than a part of the Savior.

Loretta cried as she watched her prayer of fifty-five years being answered.

Purity of confession welcomed life and light to emerge once again from the darkness of death's mine.

A few years went by ...

Now, Bill and Loretta are presently away and spending eternity together.

THE SCHOOL BELL OF
RECONCILIATION

Drunkenness results in either laughter or violence, but both result in tears. Sadly, in my life I have witnessed each effect. Violence can be spoken of later, if at all, but for now my attention rests on the laughter of alcoholism.

My great-uncle, Bob Cain, was a happy drunk for nearly all of his life. He owned an auto body shop and had a bird's nest beard, though his hair was always short and held with Brylcreem. A dab always did Uncle Bob's hair nicely, but when drinking, Uncle Bob never drank in dabs. He always drank too much, yet his laughter filled holiday cookouts and family reunions. His 1970s-style conversion van could be found in various beer gardens around town, but typically it was parked at the Blue Room. Uncle Bob was a fixture there. As a matter of fact, as a sixth grader playing football for the very first time, I was immediately granted a starting position when my coaches—also Blue Room stalwarts—found out I was Bobby Cain's nephew. I'm not sure if I possessed football prowess or not, but I was never removed from the starting lineup.

Uncle Bob's body shop was a mix between health class and an adult bookstore. I was never quite sure whether I should close my eyes for fear of divine retribution or take it all in so that I would be sufficiently, adolescently educated. Uncle Bob's world was a free-for-all. If my older sister or I had scratched our cars and needed Uncle Bob to get us out of a jam before our dad saw the damage, it was no problem. The man who held an inch of auto body paint in his lungs covered up the dings and only required a kiss as payment. My sister and I were always uncertain which was worse: kissing through the maze of Uncle Bob's beard or the anger of our dad if we confessed the auto damage. Regardless, by navigating his beard, we no longer had to be concerned with navigating an excuse for the fender bender.

As a boy, I can remember Uncle Bob would occasionally appear at our home early on Saturday mornings. My dad was a small business owner and, as he always said, "I look good on paper, but not in the pocketbook." That was no deterrent to my uncle Bob. When the doorbell rang as I was watching the first offerings of Saturday morning cartoons, my dad would always help his uncle out with whatever he could spare.

All of Uncle Bob's antics went on for years. There was always a new girlfriend, always a new commitment, and time and again Uncle Bob would swear he was never drinking. He laughed when he was drunk. We laughed when he decided to claim sobriety.

There is no happy drunk who drinks to make himself happier. Alcohol masks the pain of self-loathing, and laughter masks the folly of inebriation as acceptable medicine. When my dad's dad—my uncle Bob's brother—died, I remember Uncle Bob not even being able to enter the funeral home. The laughing man found the pain of loss too much to bear.

I loved my uncle Bob very much.

Amidst the laughter lived a crying man.

I grew up and entered the ministry.

Cain's Body Shop went out of business, and Uncle Bob retired.

Uncle Bob met a wonderful Christian lady named Wanda. Under the banner of God's love and Wanda's watchful eye, my seventy-something-year-old great uncle gained sobriety. This time none of us were surprised. This time, like none of the times before, we were proud. Still the years of alcoholism, fast living, and painting cars without a respirator held Uncle Bob like a vise. He wouldn't survive. The man who had polished auto body after auto body into perfection possessed not enough putty to put himself back together again. So we waited.

Uncle Bob was in and out of the hospital. I would always take my sons to visit their great-great-uncle. Uncle Bob loved them. When he would get home, Uncle Bob would always request my physical therapist wife to come and do his in-home therapy. After all those years of lunacy, the most stable life began to develop among us.

After some time, Wanda began attending services at my church. She would attend the early service and then leave to pick up my uncle. He would never come with her to first service but enjoyed sitting in the parking lot during second service and listening to his *Neph*, as he called me, preach on the radio. At first I asked him to just come with Wanda during first service. He never agreed, and I couldn't understand why. Yet I began to realize that while Uncle Bob was sober, and happy, and enjoyed listening to his *Neph* preach God's Word, he believed his past was far too sordid. In his heart, though he was now forever dry, he believed all of his days of drunkenness left him in place where God would never forgive him.

There is nothing sadder than a societally redeemed but broken man who sits in a church parking lot believing he is not welcome to come in and receive the love of God.

Upon realizing this, I visited my uncle over and over again and attempted to convince him of God's love and willingness to forgive. I explained to him that this is the reason Jesus died on the cross. Jesus died to come to us, to bridge the gap between all the bad we generated and all the life God desires to make ours once again. I told Uncle Bob that Jesus saying, "I am the way, and the truth, and the life; no one comes to the Father but through Me" (John 14:6 NASB), certainly declares Jesus' exclusivity as the way one passes from death to life, but it isn't a statement of exclusion to those who are, or were, the worst sinners of all. Still, though he was a faithful listener to his Rev. Neph's sermons, he would not accept the truth of reconciliation being shared with him.

Then one day I received a call from Wanda. She was afraid, and said to me, "Will you please come to your uncle Bob's house? He is really ill. I think near death, and he is refusing to allow me to call the ambulance." I jumped in my truck and was there within minutes. Lying in his holdover waterbed from the seventies, Uncle Bob weighed nearly nothing and was balled up in the fetal position. I pleaded with him to allow me to call the ambulance until finally he agreed. Wanda called 911, and I decided to offer the love of Christ to the one who had offered me so much love.

Sporting his Saviorlike beard, I simply said to my uncle, "Uncle Bob, you've heard me talk about Jesus' good news a million times. You deny none of the things from your past that still haunt you, and Jesus is unafraid to handle any of those things. He's already carried them for you. I can't make you say, yes. God loves you and wants you to receive His love. Please say, yes to Jesus and allow the Savior to lift you from the condemnation of death to the elevation of His life."

Uncle Bob said, "Yes."

I was forty years his junior, but I felt like the father who ran to receive his prodigal son home. I cried. Wanda cried. I called my dad and told him, and I think he cried too. It was a great day of genuine joy.

Uncle Bob went to the hospital and got well enough to come home for a time. After he got settled in, my wife and I went up to check on him. What Uncle Bob said to me that night ended up being prophetic.

He said, "Neph, go in there to my dining room and get that big school bell from my bell collection. Bring it in here. I need to show and tell you something."

I headed into his dining room, and in a curio cabinet of sorts were all of Uncle Bob's bells displayed. He'd been collecting them for years. I gathered the big school bell he wanted, and I took it back into the living room and gave it to him.

Holding the bell in his hands, Uncle Bob said, "Neph, I'm willing you this school bell, but I'm going to go ahead and just give it to you now. But I'm giving it to you with instructions."

I listened closely.

"I'm giving you this bell now because I'm not going to be around much longer. That church of yours is really growing, and you are going to have to build a much bigger sanctuary. I'll be long gone by then, so I need you to make me a promise."

Of course I would promise my uncle Bob anything, but I had no clue what he was talking about. Sure we were growing as a congregation and had lofty aspirations, but no one was sensing God moving us towards construction, and we hadn't even discussed with any seriousness building a new building. Still, taking the bell from him, I listened closely.

"When you build the new sanctuary, on the very first Sunday, take that school bell, go outside of the church, and ring it just like they used to ring it in the old days when they would call folks to come to church," he said.

And then with a pause, Uncle Bob said one more thing, "I want everyone to know they can welcome the gift of God's love as I have."

How could I say, no?

Uncle Bob died a few months later. Wanda asked me to officiate the funeral service, and I was honored to eulogize my favorite uncle.

Amidst our tears that day, we laughed a lot.

The funeral finished. Uncle Bob's house was sold. And Wanda brought me a copy of Uncle Bob's will to show me where Uncle Bob had willed his bell to me.

He willed me his Bible, too.

Time passed, and Uncle Bob's prophetic vision came true. My local church built a 500-seat sanctuary and planned to continue two services every Sunday. And after months and months of construction, we had our first service on Easter Sunday of 2010.

There I was outside … ringing that bell as I had promised.

Many came that Sunday.

No one sat in their cars in the parking lot.

CHAPTER IV

A TEN-YEAR-OLD'S HOPE

He smelled like corduroy and unfiltered Pall Malls. The knowledge he held was equally rough and aromatic.

Right around Halloween of 1980, my papaw died. I was ten years old. His wife, my maternal grandmother, *Granny*, was the daughter of a Methodist circuit-riding preacher. All she ever knew was church. All my papaw ever knew was the bottle and the acquisition of knowledge. He drank from the cisterns of both believing it would satiate the demonic thirsts that haunted him. There I stood, a little boy, all by myself looking at that casket that held so tightly to Papaw's lifeless body. I knew of Lazarus' resurrection, and so deep inside I cried, *Papaw, come out!* I wanted to believe Papaw was now living in the place of life but if he wasn't, then I wanted him to come on back and give life another try.

I was convinced my faith in Jesus could resurrect him, and my love could save him.

Papaw was an Appalachian sage of sorts. A smart ass amidst a world of dumb asses. Once, when I was a baby, Papaw and my mother were sitting and talking on my grandparents' back patio. Oblivious to their conversation, I was gnawing on a dirty rubber ball. Papaw said to my mother, "Nancy, get that filthy ball out of that baby's mouth!"

To which my mother replied, "Well, Daddy, don't you know they say you have to eat a peck of dirt before you die?"

To which Papaw replied, "Does the baby have to get the entire peck off of one damn ball?"

To John H. Camp, fools were not to be suffered even when the foolish branches were from one's own family tree.

While I don't remember the peck-of-dirt-in-one-sitting incident, I do remember another afternoon on their back patio when I was preschool age. Papaw was speaking of West Virginia's senators at the time, Senators Randolph and Byrd (at one point of Papaw's life, he was a speechwriter for Senator Byrd). I was listening and so I asked, "Who are Senators Randolph and Byrd?" Papaw was appalled I had not yet received my first civics lesson. Regardless of my preschool standing, right then and there my training in the intricacies of the United States government commenced.

Papaw was so intelligent and held so much knowledge about so many things his presence brought intimidation. He was also a big man, nearly 6'4", and more than 200 pounds. He was the perfect storm. Tall, lean, with a Mensa IQ all wrapped in a liquor bottle, Papaw led a life that typically resulted in violence.

Not as a child but definitely as I grew older, I heard of the times Papaw would hit my granny so hard it would tip the chair over she was sitting in. I was told of a night Papaw got in a bar fight, had his jaw broken, and instead of going to the emergency room to have his jaw reset, Papaw came home and headed to the bathroom with a fifth of Jack Daniel's to perform oral and maxillofacial surgery on himself. My mom told me Papaw and bar fights were the norm. Papaw would get drunk, bring to light a dumb ass's ignorance, and then the fists would begin flying. Mom said her brother, my uncle Dave, was picking Papaw up from a bar after a fight nearly every weekend.

Everything came to a head in 1976. It was Christmas, and my older sister and I had spent that particular Friday night with Granny at her house. I don't recall whether or not Papaw was there. I do remember it was snowing that Saturday morning when we woke up. After breakfast, Granny loaded us into her red-and-black Maverick and drove us across our little town to our house on Carolina Avenue.

My dad and mom had been building a new home a few blocks away from our current home, but the contractor was taking forever. I had no idea this particular snowy Saturday before Christmas of 1976 would be the Saturday when we were moving. As we pulled up to our Carolina Avenue home, instead of going inside we were rerouted to our West Park Avenue new house by my parents and their friends who were helping them move.

I'm not sure which I was more excited about: Christmas snow or a new house.

That day is a blur, but at the end of it something strange happened. When it was time for everyone to go home everyone did go home, except for my granny. Saturday nights were her Sunday school lesson preparation nights, so we were never allowed to spend the night on Saturday. From that context, rarely did we ever even visit with Granny on Saturday nights. Yet, there she remained within our home, about to spend the night with us.

I wasn't sure why.

I began to wonder, *Where is Papaw?*

One Saturday night turned into months. Granny wasn't sleeping over … *she was moving in.* Papaw was nowhere to be found. My sister and I didn't see him nor even know where he was. It was all very strange. Then my mother sat down with my older sister and me to share with us some hard words concerning Papaw.

Keely was eight-years-old.

I was six.

Mom said, "Your papaw is really sick, and you're not going to be able to see him for a while." This was something I didn't want to hear. I'm not sure I even looked at Keely to see her third-grade response. Mom continued, saying, "I need you all to do one thing for me. Make me this promise. If your papaw drives by and tries to pick you up when you're walking home from school or out playing, don't get in the car with him. Just run home."

No little boy or girl should ever have to hear those words concerning their papaw.

My mom wasn't trying to hurt us. She was trying to protect us from the hurt she had experienced so many times herself.

Keely and I didn't know this papaw. Most certainly, the papaw we knew smoked in the house and didn't go to church, but in those days that wasn't uncommon. The papaw we knew rode us around in his tractor, taught Keely how to ride a bike, and took us down to the funeral home where he worked from time to time and walked us through the casket room. The papaw we knew sat on the back patio with us in the summertime and ate Fiddle-Faddle and Bugles while listening to the Pittsburgh Pirates games on the AM radio while Granny was stringing green beans from their garden. The papaw we knew reminded us of John Wayne, not some monster we couldn't get in the car with. We never believed papaw would hurt us because we had never seen nor heard of him hurting anyone else.

Those testimonies all began to come forth.

Week after week, Sunday after Sunday, summer after summer, I would sit in Sunday school classrooms, sanctuaries, and Vacation Bible School hearing of Christ's love and how Jesus died on the cross and rose from the dead so everyone could be saved. The preacher told me that. My mother told me that. Granny prepared every single Saturday night to tell her high school Sunday school class that. All I could think of was, *If it is good enough for all of us, then why isn't it good enough for Papaw?*

I began praying for Papaw every single night.

I would always say, "Lord, bless Papaw. Mom says he's sick, but I pray that he will get better. I love Granny living with us, but I want to spend the night at their house once again. Please heal him. Please forgive him. Please tell Papaw you love him."

These were the prayers I prayed for over a year.

I don't know the intricacies, the battles, nor all of the negotiations in between, but sometime in 1978 Granny moved back to her home. Keely and I began spending the night with Papaw and Granny once again.

Papaw's brother, Bill Camp, was a preacher. He pastored Woodland United Methodist Church in Morgantown, West Virginia, on the east side of the Monongahela River. While I never remember Papaw ever attending Westover United Methodist Church on the west side of the Mon River, he did begin faithfully attending his brother's church. Week after week Papaw went to church and helped with the sound system as he listened to his brother, Bill, preach the Gospel. It was having an effect, or at least Keely and I thought so.

Papaw seemed peaceful. It was like the tension had slipped away. Whether Papaw's conversion and its results were real or we simply desired it to be real, Keely and I could feel Papaw's peace when he hugged us into all that corduroy and tobacco smell.

Papaw never quit smoking.

Then, in the midst of all the peace and reconciliation, the family curse struck. It was a rare blood disease that both my great-uncle Bill and my papaw developed. Because I was a boy I do not remember the particulars, but I do remember both of them requiring constant blood transfusions.

Uncle Bill succumbed to the disease first.

It was a Sunday morning. Uncle Bill had just finished his sermon and was giving the altar call. The Singing Koon Family had taken their place up front to sing, "Pass Me Not O' Gentle Savior." As Uncle Bill opened the altars for people to come and receive life, his body collapsed to the floor. Uncle Bill had given up his spirit, and Papaw ran to take his brother's empty body in his arms.

Papaw was soon to follow.

Papaw had been sick for a while. If I remember correctly, a makeshift hospital room had been set up in my grandparents' dining room. The man who was once a hulking figure of intelligence and strength was fading away. His wit and newfound love were not.

It was October of 1980, right around Halloween. It was after school and I was heading up two blocks to my best buddy's house to play Nerf football.

The phone rang, and somehow I just knew. No one needed to tell me, though they did. Papaw was gone. I just sat on the couch and looked out the window at all those beautiful leaves of red, orange, and gold. They were dying. He was dead. Just like Papaw, they would soon be dead, too.

So there I stood. In the same funeral home where I have now officiated hundreds of funerals as a preacher, that evening so long ago I stood as a ten-year-old boy eyeing up my papaw's dead body. All alone at the casket, I truly believed that my faith could raise him from the dead. I looked and looked for any sign of life, but none came.

I will always remember where I was seated during the funeral. I was sitting directly behind my uncle Dave, my papaw's only son. As the hymns played, the Scriptures were read, and Rev. Stacey Grosscup eulogized my papaw, my uncle Dave cried uncontrollably. I can still see him shaking. I had never seen a man cry before.

Papaw was buried in the Burnt Meeting House Cemetery in Harmony Grove, West Virginia. It was on the site of his family's farm.

For the last thirty-seven years I have thought about my papaw and whether or not he received the reconciling love of Christ. After my granny died a few years ago, my mother alone, as the only living child, took the responsibility of going through Papaw and Granny's house. While doing so, my mother found a number of letters Granny had written. My mother said some could be easily disregarded, but most of what her mother wrote concerning her dad is horribly painful to read. Jesus teaches that as we forgive, so we will be forgiven. Suffice to say, the letters reveal that her mother, my granny, had to forgive her father, my papaw, of much.

Granny lived her life standing with Christ, offered forgiveness to all, and has been forgiven as well. That truth is easily reconciled. Yet, to forgive a man who caused so much pain is an entirely different undertaking.

There is one more letter though in Granny's handwriting that my mother found. It is a letter that speaks of my Granny's joy upon seeing Papaw's conversion to Christ. While there may be equals, there is no one person in the world who knew of Christ's reconciling love more than Granny. If she has testified as to Papaw's conversion, then none have the moral authority to contradict her.

But what of the pain Papaw left behind?

Of course my sister and I are willing to see Papaw as a changed man, but until we had been told he was dangerous, we had seen him only as the rough riding urban cowboy we believed him to be. We never witnessed the violence. We never were embarrassed by the infidelity. We were never cut so deeply that we would emotionally scar. We never watched him strike our mother as a daughter, knocking her over in a chair.

So perhaps this testimony is not so much about my papaw's salvation as it is for those who need to hear Jesus' words that say, "I am the One Who forgives much, because I have been hurt much. I am the One Who heals greatly, because I have received the deepest wounds. I am the One Who loves mightily, because I have been hated greatly. I know your anger. I know your hurt. I know your wounds. I know your hatred. Allow me to love you. All things will be made new."

CHAPTER V

AND FORREST WALKS WITH GOD

It is recorded in Genesis 5:24, "Enoch walked faithfully with God; then he was no more, because God took him away."

Not a bad way to go.

Enoch is not alone in his favored passing. Jacob, after blessing his sons, draws his knees into his chest, breathes his last, and is gathered unto his people. Elijah is swooped up in a golden, fiery chariot. Steven, while being pummeled by stones, sees Jesus, the Son standing at the right hand of God the Father, and then drifts off to sleep. Perhaps this is too much of a nursery rhyme view of the means by which some Biblical figures pass from this world to the next, but whether in the Bible or the world before us, God uses the means of a man's passing to bring about the truth of God's reconciling love. It was in the passing of my father-in-law, Forrest Cloonan, I experienced this truth most vividly.

Forrest's daughter, Lesley—my wife—is the only girl I have ever dated. She is the only girl I have ever kissed. The two of us, after twenty-six years of marriage to date, have been milling around one another since somewhere in the vicinity of 1983. I was an eighth grader and she was a seventh grader, though only two months separate our birthdays.

Now, no father is looking forward to the first teenage boy to come a-courting his daughter. Forrest was no exception. While he was polite, welcoming, and never pointed a shotgun at me upon my initial arrival, it was clear he was just fine if I chose not to hang around too long.

But I didn't go away.

Frankly, I knew early on I wanted to marry his daughter. That might sound strange for an eighth grader to know his matrimonial plans, but somewhere deep inside I knew I was going to marry Forrest Cloonan's daughter one day.

Did I mention Forrest was a retired captain in the United States federal prison system?

Well, when his daughter and I began dating it was the Reagan eighties, and I was more intent on being Sonny Crockett of Miami Vice fame than a good boyfriend. Both Forrest and his wife brought to my attention the fact that I was wearing no socks with my shoes as I picked their daughter up for the ninth grade dance. I didn't back down, and soon after I found myself on the other end of the phone with an angry and fed up father.

"Don't you ever call my daughter again, young man," Forrest said.

I replied, "We'll see about that!" Then I hung up on Federal Prison Captain Forrest Cloonan. It is not one of my prouder moments.

Months later recognizing my utter failure, I worked up the nerve one Saturday night to dial the Cloonans' phone number.

"Hello," Lesley said as I thanked the Lord she had answered.

"Hey, Les," I said in return.

"Who's this?"

My stomach dropped. My facade was confidence, but my reality was fear and intimidation. I began to lower the phone back to the receiver, never to call Lesley Cloonan again, when all of a sudden something inside me cried out, *This is the girl you love. Say something, you fool!*

Putting the phone back to my ear, I said, "It's Kevin."

In an instant, Lesley wrangled up a high school friend with a car and the two headed to my house without her parents' knowledge. When Lesley finally broke it to her parents that she and I were a thing again, I was required to come and formally apologize to the Cloonans for my phone antics from a few months prior and to endure a lecture from my elders.

I didn't mind.

Frankly, I knew I deserved it.

Mostly on, but for a few short stints off, Lesley and I have been together ever since.

Over the years, Forrest and I became dear friends. I enjoyed holidays and cookouts with my in-laws, going on jaunts in Southern West Virginia to Forrest's old stomping grounds of Pocahontas County, and some of our best times occurred when Forrest and I painted quite a few rooms together while Lesley and I were building our first home. Forrest was never short on opinions, and most of the time they were comedic.

On one occasion, as the two of us began painting our living room, Forest questioned his daughter's choice of paint color, saying, "What in *thee* Hell is the color of this paint?"

I answered him, saying, "The color is called *fool's gold*."

Forrest huffed and simply said, "Well, I can tell why they named it that. Only a fool would paint her walls this color."

With Forrest it was like that all the time.

When Lesley was buying her first car, I wanted to take Forrest out in my mother's car, which was the same model Lesley would be buying. I was driving. Forrest was sitting in the front seat of the passenger side. I was going over all the safety features and said to Forrest, "There is an air bag on both the driver's side and the passenger's side."

Forrest huffed again and said, "I've been driving around with a passenger side airbag for thirty-five years."

Forrest always made us laugh, even if it was at my mother-in-law's expense.

One evening Lesley and I and her parents had gone to dinner at a local Italian restaurant. As we returned to their split-level house, my mother-in-law excused herself to go to the restroom. Lesley, Forrest, and I continued our conversation. After some time, my mother-in-law emerged from the bathroom and was greeted by Forrest saying, "My

God, woman. It smells like something died down there. Can you please do something about that smell!"

The two were affectionately known as *the Bickersons*, so Ann was giving it back to Forrest just as heartily as she headed back to tend to the aroma.

When she returned I was minding my p's and q's, saying nothing at all. Ann sat in her chair. Forrest sat in his. Lesley and I were on the couch. No one said a word to break the silence.

I regressed to the ninth grade all of a sudden, knowing it was not my place to break the ice.

My mother-in-law turned to my father-in-law and said, "What?"

"You know what," Forrest said.

Pursing her lips, Ann shot back, saying, "I don't know what!"

Forrest just shook his head up and down, cleared something from his eyetooth with his tongue, and with a perfect dramatic pause he finally said, "Well, that's just great. Now it smells like shit and potpourri."

It was always like this. They adored one another, and they certainly loved their daughter and their grandsons, but there were not too many religious discussions going on with their preacher son-in-law. And there was a reason for that.

While Forrest and Ann were quite respectful of my calling to ministry, they did not attend any local church. There was a great deal of pain from their past, and like so many who have suffered personal loss upon personal loss, Forrest and Ann were wounded warriors. Forrest had suffered a massive heart attack years prior, and he was left with only a portion of a functioning heart. Ann's father suddenly passed away before she had ever reached her teens. A few decades later, Ann's mother died of Alzheimer's disease and breast cancer. Then, adding to the pain, Ann developed breast cancer and was forced to undergo a mastectomy. She nearly died.

Disease, death, and divine questions left the Cloonans punch drunk and unable to answer the call of the Sunday morning church bells. They weren't averse to Christianity. Forrest, like so many Appalachian men, grew up believing but didn't go with regularity. Ann, to her credit, grew up more than active in the Presbyterian Church and even became the organist. The Cloonans possessed deep respect, but they were tired, wounded, and justifiably had their share of Job-like questions.

It went on like this for years, and then came the spring of 1998. Forrest had been diagnosed with prostate cancer, and while the issue was serious, it didn't seem to be life threatening. Forrest was receiving treatments and actually had a new doctor who was a bit older than I, but with whom I, as a little boy, had actively gone to the same Sunday school. That day in the spring of 1998 was the first day Forrest had an appointment with my doctoring friend.

The appointment went well, but later in the day Forrest started talking without making sense. Ann immediately took Forrest to the emergency room. Lesley called me, and I hurried to the hospital as fast as I could after securing our two toddler sons with my parents.

By the time I got to the hospital Forrest had already been admitted, and he had already undergone a series of full-body scans to determine whether the cancer had spread. I stepped off the elevator and there was my friend, now Forrest's doctor, eye-to-eye with me. I could see he was stunned.

I questioned him, saying, "Doc, what is it?"

He just shook his head.

We walked in Forrest's room together where Ann and Lesley were waiting by Forrest's bedside.

"I have bad news," my friend said. He continued to give the diagnosis, saying, "There's no sense in skirting the reality. Mr. Cloonan, you have what we believe to be an inoperable malignant brain tumor."

Even if we had wanted to, no one spoke a word. We thought Forrest was simply dealing with a manageable form of prostate cancer, and then this … another tragedy. Lesley and her mother stepped out of the room to talk with the doctors.

Forrest and I were left in stunned silence alone.

I stood there forever, trying to stand by Forrest's side while Ann and

Lesley were peppering a now growing number of doctors with questions. I had no words to say. I had stood in hundreds of hospital rooms with equally bad news, but this time it was *my* father-in-law and friend. Scared to death, I did the only thing I knew to do.

"Forrest," I said.

Looking away to someplace far beyond where we presently were, Forrest said, "Yes?"

I just kept going, saying, "I've never pushed my Christianity on you before, but brother, this is life and death. I have to ask you: do you believe in Jesus as your Lord and Savior?"

Forrest's answer was simple and honest. He said, "You know, Kevin, I haven't gone to church like I should have over the years, but yes, I believe in Jesus as my Lord and Savior."

Through my tears I said to my brother-in-Christ, "Let's just pray and seal the deal, and we will never have to be concerned with this again."

I bought Forrest a Bible, and he read just as long as he could. The brain tumor took over, though, and six weeks later there we were holding hands around Forrest's intensive care room bed, waiting for him to head home.

I was there, Lesley was there, her mother was there, and some of our dearest friends in the world were there. The nurse told us, "It won't be long."

We were crying quietly, and no one said a thing. In my heart I began to sing some old hymns, probably many of the same ones Ann played in her Presbyterian church as a young girl.

Then, unbeknownst to everyone in that room, inside my soul rose the still small voice of God, saying, *And Forrest walks with God.*

Our caring nurse said, "He's gone."

CHAPTER VI

BURYING *INSERT NAME OF FAMOUS MUSICIAN HERE*

Some better-left-unsaid stories just have to be told.

When I interview families prior to eulogizing their deceased loved ones, invariably every family, in one form or another, tells me that their mother, their father, their husband, their wife, their friend, "would give anything to anyone in need." Jesus Himself, as recorded in Matthew 25, declares that such character is the evidence for preparedness for His return. The tale you are about to read is not only the testimony of a giving woman, but also a picture of the greedy, divisive, and comedically sad chaos that sometimes surrounds funeral visitations, funerals, and committal services.

A request of Jesus was once made by a wolfish family member, who said, "Teacher, tell my brother to divide the family inheritance with me." (Luke 12:13 NASB) To which Jesus replied, "Man, who appointed Me a judge or arbitrator over you?" (Luke 12:14 NASB) Disputes at the funeral home and the graveside are common occurrences, even when the deceased matriarch lived her life giving anything to anyone in need.

I offer this story in no way making light of any family's grief, but to deny the insatiable madness behind those who are divvying up earthly treasures at the expense of others and fighting amongst themselves even before the casket has been covered with sod would be an equal crime. If the following story weren't so true, it would be sad. In the midst of the lunacy, it just might be both.

The phone rang.

"Hello," I said.

My funeral director buddy was on the other end of the line, saying, "What are you doing Saturday?"

I knew why he was calling but wasn't ready to commit, so I questioned him, saying, "Why do you ask?"

Verbally volleying, my funeral director friend said slyly, "You want to bury *Insert Name of Famous Musician Here*?"

The name my funeral director friend gave me was one of the most famous musical artists this world knows. Obviously I cannot share the name of the deceased nor the musician, or else the innocent would not be protected. Still, the fact that the deceased shares a name with a famous musician makes the incident both more silly and surreal.

"Noooo waay," I said, dragging out the words.

Letting me down easy, he said, "Now, it's not *thee Insert Name of Famous Musician Here*, but you still have some information to work with."

Officiating a funeral service for a family and eulogizing a person, none of whom you have ever met, is intimidating. With every funeral, any pastor who truly cares wants to bring glory and honor to God, declaration of Christ, tribute to the deceased, and compassion to the grieving family. Where there is little to no information concerning the deceased, this is the most difficult of tasks.

I thought it over for a moment, and while it wasn't *thee Insert Name of Famous Musician Here*, there was a family in need, and I could help, so I agreed.

He gave me the times of the visitation and funeral and said, "It'll be easy. She has five children, and she was a nurse on a life-flight helicopter. You should be able to get some good stories from that."

I told my friend I would see him Friday at 2:00 p.m., one hour prior to the first visitation.

Friday came, and with note-taking journal and pen in hand, I headed to the funeral home. When I got there, a crowd was already assembled.

I headed up the front walk and into the stone funeral home, where I sat in the funeral director's office and waited for the family to finish their initial time by themselves paying their respects over the deceased.

Unless I know the family well, I never follow them in for the family viewing. It is time for them to be together making sure everything is just right, to look at the flower arrangements, and to set out all the pictures that help to recall the greatest of memories. It doesn't take long for families to settle in. They've already dealt with so much grief. Still, each step when losing a loved one is a journey, and thus preachers must be sensitive to death's pilgrimage.

I was casually talking with the funeral home staff when I looked up and found three of the deceased's children standing in the doorway and perched with a question.

A middle-aged woman in jeans and a blouse asked me, "Are you the preacher?"

"I am," I said, then asked, "Are you the deceased's daughter?"

The woman said she was and that the man and the woman with her were her brother and sister. I remembered the funeral director telling me there were five siblings, but I was only seeing three.

I asked, "Can we sit and talk about the particulars of the service, or are we still waiting on your other siblings?"

There was an uncomfortable silence, before the woman finally answered, saying, "The other two won't be here until the seven o'clock visitation."

Late arriving family was not uncommon, so as the woman took a seat among us, I opened my journal, clicked my pen, and said as I always do, "I don't want you walking out of here tomorrow saying, 'I wish Kevin would have said *this* about Mom.' You tell me the *this* and I will put it all together for you."

No one answered. There was not a word from the woman who had been talking nor her siblings standing stoically behind her. I was quickly realizing this simple funeral was not going to be so simple.

I asked, "Tell me about your mother."

The woman said, "She was a wonderful lady."

Then there was dead silence.

So I questioned, saying, "Did your mother have any hobbies?"

With no help from brother nor sister, the same woman said, "She loved watching television."

I turned to the funeral director and gritted my teeth a bit as if to say, *Thanks a lot.*

So I went to the surefire bit of information and asked, "I see from the obituary that your mother was a nurse on a life-flight helicopter."

Almost in chorus, the three siblings exploded together, saying, "It's a lie! Our sister is nothing but a liar."

I now understood why three of the siblings were attending the 3:00 to 5:00 visitation, and the other two siblings would be attending the 7:00 to 9:00 visitation. I was in the middle of the war between three siblings and two. I quickly regrouped and began walking down through the names of family members listed in the obituary. I began asking if any of their mother's siblings were there. The deceased had a number of siblings.

I asked, "Is your mother's sister here?"

"Yes," they said.

Next on the list of surviving siblings of the deceased was a brother named Vince, so I asked, "And your mother's brother, Vince... is your uncle Vince here?"

"No, Vince is not here. He's dead!"

Apparently this was another lie. I scratched out Vince's name from the list of survivors and moved him to the category titled, "Preceded In Death."

This line of questioning went on for ten or fifteen minutes until before my eyes the siblings kind of just dispersed. I wasn't even exactly sure where they went. Perhaps they had drifted to the front porch of the funeral home while I was looking down and scribbling in my journal some fragment of information I was going to attempt to use to form an acceptable eulogy. I decided to search for them on the porch where cigarette smoke had settled in like a fog bank.

I honestly have no problem with people smoking around me. While I never smoked, plenty of people I know do, so I have become oblivious to cigarette smoke. Yet, on the front porch of the funeral home had congregated a number of smokers rivaling a Marlboro convention. Through the haze of nicotine exhaust, I relocated the daughter who had been attempting to answer my questions.

As I approached her, an older man walked out from the funeral home and onto the porch. Wearing his funeral suit and hobbling on a cane, he was an enhancing fixture to the assembly I found myself congregated among.

As the family saw him, a collective shout went up, "Vince!"

I was confused. Certainly this wasn't the deceased's "Preceded In Death brother Vince." The three non-free-flow-of-information brother and sisters had reported to me of Vince's demise. So I walked up and introduced myself to the heralded man.

I said, "Hello, sir. I'm the preacher who will be officiating the funeral tomorrow. You seem like a popular guy. What's your name?"

I was expecting him to answer, "Lazarus," or "The widow of Nain's son," but in no way whatsoever was I expecting him to tell me his name was "Uncle Vince."

With the most straightforward answer I had received to date, the man said, "I'm the deceased's brother, Vince."

Inside I cried, *Hallelujah!* Vince was resurrected from the dead, and my funeral director buddy who had assured me this would be an easy funeral was about to be murdered. Hoping to hear the bell that ended the round, I headed inside to try to find the deceased's sister.

Sitting in the second row from the casket holding not-thee-*Insert Name Here of Famous Musician*'s body was an older lady who I recognized. Though I did not know her name, she was at least a familiar face. Tapping me on the shoulder and whispering in my ear, a member of the funeral home staff pointed to the woman and said, "That's the deceased's sister." I made a beeline for her.

"Hello, Preacher," the woman said as I sat down in the first row directly in front of her.

"It's good to see a familiar face," I said. "I'm very sorry about your sister."

She pulled some tattered Kleenex from the sleeve of her dress, blew her nose, and said, "Thank you. I'm just going to miss my sister."

Even among the circus outside, I was broken for this woman who longed for her sister.

I asked, "I'm trying to get any information concerning your sister for the funeral tomorrow. Are there any particulars about her you can share with me?"

With a good hearty sniff, the woman said, "You know my sister was just the most wonderful person in the world. She would do anything for anybody. As a matter of fact, if she had a loaf of bread and saw someone in need, she would give three-quarters of the loaf to that person and keep half for herself."

I did my best not to laugh out loud, but even with my limited math abilities, *Insert Name Here of Famous Musician*'s sister's numbers just didn't add up. I clicked my pen closed, shut my journal, and headed home to cry.

The next day was equally spectacular.

The siblings didn't speak.

There was an argument of what was to be left in and what was to come out from the casket.

And as I led the pallbearers carrying the coffin of the not-so-famous to the hearse, one of the pallbearers decided it would be best to adorn himself with a sleeveless "Goldberg" t-shirt.

Yes.

You heard me correctly.

I said, "Goldberg," the wrestler from WWE fame.

You can't make this stuff up.

The funeral procession was a long one. We traveled somewhere near 40 miles to a cemetery in which I had never been before nor ever visited again. I completed my committal service, and then stepped to the side so the funeral home staff could offer their standard final tribute.

Some representative from the funeral home always recited a monologue concerning how a white dove has been the symbol of the Spirit for thousands of years, while one of the funeral home staff held said white dove in his hands, poised to release it as the recitation concluded. In this instance, it was my friend the funeral director giving the speech and his brother-in-law was readied to release the dove. As my friend finished by saying, "We symbolically release her spirit back to God on the wings of a dove," his brother-in-law then released the white dove into the air.

The family loved it. Every family does. Frankly, the dove release is a nice gesture and closes the service with hope.

As my friend dismissed everyone to their cars, he and I headed towards his brother-in-law to call an end to this funeral fiasco.

When we reached his brother-in-law, he was covering his hand and in obvious distress. The funeral director and I both said, "What's wrong? What happened?" His brother-in-law removed his hand from the other, revealing a mangled hand dripping with blood.

"What in the world?"

The funeral director's brother-in-law said, "The dove attacked me."

Looking up, the dove of peace and light had decided to change its course. It wasn't interested in our symbolic gesture of compassion. It was returning for another run. Right there in that cemetery the dove of peace and light started dive bombing us all.

81

We ran for the hearse and the hills. I'd never seen anything like it before, and I've never seen anything like it since.

Every family we care for is different. Some are kind and sacrificial. Others are selfish and greedy. Every family gets one chance to say a final goodbye. It is my prayer that every family would cease from crying, "Make my siblings divide the inheritance with me!" It is my prayer that in the face of loss everyone would come together and esteem everyone better than himself.

Appalachian Eulogies: The *This* to Be Remembered

CHAPTER I

A MOTHER-IN-LAW AND HER DAUGHTER'S HUSBAND

When I showed up at the Cloonans' home for the first time as a fourteen-year-old kid, I'm positive neither Forrest nor Ann Cloonan believed they were being introduced to the young man who would be both marrying their daughter and eulogizing their lives. That evening I was simply a ninth-grader who had come to escort their daughter to the end-of-year spring dance. That was 1985, and for the next thirty-one years I would be occasionally out but mostly in the life of the Cloonan family.

On May 9, 1992, Ann Cloonan became my mother-in-law when I became her daughter's husband. As you will read in the eulogy that follows, Ann and I disagreed many times. More honestly stated, we had our share of fights. Yet, over the twenty-four years I was married to Ann's only child, she and I battled through our disharmony to become dear friends.

Relationships are more easily walked away from than fought for. Between Ann and me was a beautiful lady whom we both loved more than anything and anyone else. According to blood, Lesley was Ann's heredity. According to Scripture, Lesley was flesh of my flesh and bone of my bone. I had left father and mother, was joined to Lesley, and the two of us had become one. Ann always struggled to let go. I always struggled to share. Before Ann's death, this mother-in-law and her daughter's husband became friends.

It was a Friday morning in August when our oldest and our youngest sons found Ann's body leaning over in her chair. Our youngest had just passed his driver's license test and wanted to tell his grandma Ann he could now drive to see her any time. She didn't answer when he called. The two boys went to Ann's home to share the news of the passed driver's test and to check on their grandma Ann who wasn't answering her phone. Soon all three grandsons, daughter, and son-in-law were there crying, praying, and considering the words of the final goodbye.

I eulogized my dear friend the following Tuesday.

The eulogy of Ann Cloonan

Eulogizing people you don't know is difficult because you know nothing about them but easy because there is no emotional connection.

Eulogizing people you do know is easy because you know so much about them you could tell stories for days, but it is difficult because you love them.

I have known Ann Cloonan for three quarters of my forty-five-plus years. Nearly thirty-two of those forty-five-plus years I have been in love with Ann's only child. In the beginning, I was just another little boy who was dialing 292-7443 and hoping to navigate my way past the fatherly protection of the federal prison guard. Yet Forrest was the smaller of the two towers that had to be climbed to get to my Rapunzel. The tower Forrest had constructed was made up of old stone, but I found that if I spoke respectfully to the initially gruff man guarding the castle door, then his hardened jaw would be transformed into a gentle, welcoming smile.

Then there was Ann.

I was the boy who had shown up to take away her Cinderella, her Sleeping Beauty, her Little Mermaid. What I met with was not fairy godmother. Frankly, to me, Ann was more Maleficent. For two decades it was an arduous journey, but in the end I came to know Ann as an intricate quilt, a beautiful tole painting, and a glorious song played on a Presbyterian pipe organ.

Ann Cloonan was a medical transcriptionist. Ann was an artist. Ann was a woman who loved and was proud of her Southern West Virginia home and heritage. In many ways, Ann was a demander of excellence. Much of the time Ann was honest without a filter, but she was always grateful.

Ann was Job.

Ann loved Forrest. She loved her grandsons. She loved her daughter. And while it was always a little difficult for her to say to her son-in-law, and for her son-in-law to say to her, Ann loved her son-in-law very much ... and he loved her very much, too.

This is the Ann Cloonan I know, and this is the Ann Cloonan I would like to honor today.

The first time I saw Ann was at a Westover Elementary School Fall Festival. I'm not even sure why I remember this, but it was on the second floor of the old Westover Elementary located on Morrison Avenue here in Westover. Each year, the PTO, faculty, and staff of Westover Elementary would kick off the school year with a festival of games, food, prizes, and a haunted house. Like so many others I had attended, and as I ventured upstairs to Mrs. Wilson's fifth-grade classroom, a jolly, gray-haired lady I had never seen before was wo-manning one of the game stations. My immediate connection with Ann would last only as long as the time of the game, but her impact upon me in those moments is just as alive today as it was in that wood-floored classroom from thirty-five years ago. Little did I know that the animated woman who was handing me darts to toss at balloons for a prize would one day be my mother-in-law.

I finished the game and took my prize. I turned to the door, and Ann turned to the next little boy in line. A few years later, now at Westover

Junior High, a pretty little saxophone-playing girl from Pleasant Hills walked into the band room. I didn't know she was the only daughter and only child of that woman from the fall festival I had encountered a few years prior, but even at that young age I knew I wanted to be part of the Cloonan family's life forever and ever.

Quickly I came to know that Ann and Forrest were proud members of our country's labor force. Forrest was captain of the prison guard at the Kennedy Center, and Ann was a polished and proficient medical transcriptionist for Ruby Memorial Hospital and for Drs. Holehouse and Rollins. In her retirement, Ann decided to come out of retirement and be the office manager of sorts for an internal medicine physician, Dr. Wren. Looking back, I remember Ann working countless hours with those earphones in her ears. She was either typing at her desk in her basement or heading to the hospital to feverishly dance her fingers across a keyboard. Ann typed doctors' notes and dissertations for doctors and doctoral students alike. She was thorough, grammatically sound, and well respected. Day and night I can remember Ann either heading to or coming home from the workplace. The wisdom of Proverbs 31 declares that the virtuous woman never eats the bread of idleness. As Ann labored among the workforce, the loaves of laziness were never present upon her table.

Ann's typewriters and computer terminals were the tools of her labors, but the adornment of her home were her quilts and her paintings. It is the paintings I remember first. Ann was a tole painter. Now, if you are not familiar with this Appalachian art form, Tole painting is the folk art of decorative painting on tin and wooden utensils, objects and furniture. Ann was a master at the craft and not only shared her gift with others by providing pieces of art to folks, Ann also taught others this Americana art form. The first time, and every time, I went to the Cloonans' home, there was always a door hanging Forrest had cut out with his jigsaw and Ann had tole-painted. Typically it was a piece of art to honor the season, but throughout Forrest and Ann's home were paintings of Abraham and Sara, intricately painted boxes and plates, and Appalachian landscapes that had been crafted by Ann's hands. The Scriptures teach us that out of the abundance of the heart a person's mouth speaks. The Appalachia Ann adored in her heart flowed to her hands, and those hands painted the beauty of the West Virginia hills all of us know to be so majestic and so grand. For the casual, Ann's paintings were ramshackle outhouses and simple flowers, but for those who were willing to stop and look they could see the very breeze in the trees blowing over Ann's crossroads towns of Hillsboro and Marlinton. As a junior high kid I certainly did not appreciate such artistic craft, but through the years, like her many other students, Ann taught me a deeper appreciation of our wild, wonderful West Virginia.

In her later years, Ann began quilting. She had probably made many quilts as a girl. No one who was as polished a quilter as Ann was could have picked up the craft with such excellence, but it seemed as Lesley moved into womanhood, Ann's passion for painting transitioned into quilting all the more strongly. Ann was known in every fabric shop and quilters guild throughout the state. Featherweight sewing machines are in tiny black boxes throughout Ann's home. I remember countless weekend trips she and Forrest would take to go buy another Featherweight sewing machine nestled in some nook and cranny of some backwoods West Virginia holler. She taught us that the proficiency of a quilter is to be determined by the amount of stitches per inch. The more precision stitches per inch, the better the quilter. As a quilter, and in life, Ann Cloonan had many precision stitches per inch.

Hopefully, you can hear from my characterization of Ann that she lived her life as a very proud West Virginian. Now, my mother had mountain toys scattered throughout our home. We took trips to Pipestem, Hawks Nest, Seneca Rocks, and the Cassville Railroad as children. Part of me believes Coopers Rock is part of my family's home-place. Yet, in Ann and Forrest Cloonan, I received the beautiful opportunity to share life with people who love this great state as much as my mom.

Until the Cloonans welcomed me into their life, I had driven through Summersville and stopped at the Summersville Dairy Queen, but I had no idea of the beautiful hands that were surrounding that pass-through,

Southern West Virginia city. As we would pass over Summersville Mountain in the Cloonans' brown Ford Taurus, or blue Ford Tempo, or that green Ford minivan (Forrest had a thing for Fords—which reminds me of a time we hit a skunk, but that's another story for another day—I digress). As we would pass over Summersville Mountain, Forrest would always make a left towards Muddlety, or Richwood, or Nettie, and I found myself in the wonder of Marlinton, Hillsboro, Greenbank, Lewisburg, and the Greenbrier Valley.

I found it interesting while I was typing the names of these cities, the spell-check on my computer underlined all the towns in red. The world may not know of West Virginia's beauty, but Forrest and Ann taught me that their home is anything but a typo. With Forrest and Ann, I saw hills prettier than those I saw in Austria. I ate pies nearly as good as my grandma Dot's. And I can tell you I have been to the Louvre in Paris twice, and the Louvre doesn't have anything on Lesley's Grandpa Jake's house. Forrest and Ann introduced me to DNR trappers and a World War II veteran named Punk. I got to cross the Scenic Highway with Forrest and Ann, and they took me to Droop Mountain Battlefield. I would come home and proudly tell my mom where Forrest and Ann had taken me. I had found two people who loved West Virginia as much as she did. Yes, some people see West Virginia as a typo but not my mom, and not Forrest and not Ann. They love West Virginia, and I love it more and more because of them. Lesley's dream is to one day, in our retirement, live on the Buckeye Road, but because of our parents' love for country roads that take us home, both of us are going to make sure our retirement will be spent on the West Virginia side.

Now, at this point allow me to speak of Ann's commitment to excellence, honesty, lack of filter, and her gratefulness. If you have ever been to a shoe store with Ann, you may have heard her say, "You cannot buy those shoes. Your ankles are too fat." If you've ever been to Bob Evans, then there is a strong chance you have heard her lecture the Bob Evans staff regarding their food quality, inconsiderate choice of seating for the handicapped among us, and/or their need for personal grooming. There are also a few of us (note I said "us") who have heard, "Let me tell you what I really think about you!" And if you have ever been on the receiving end of Ann's reprimand for losing Volume Seven from her *Encyclopedia Britannica* set or after taking a bite from Ann's dinner roll, then you know Ann could be brutally honest to a fault. I'm not going to lie: Ann hurt my feelings on more than one occasion, but if we can cut through the barbs, what Ann was demanding was excellence. She was a leader. She was an artist. As a medical transcriptionist, Ann corrected doctors' dictation mistakes so people's lives would be healed, preserved, and strengthened. Yes, sometimes Ann was a bit rude with her opinions, but when you love someone you learn to develop a filter for her criticism even when she chooses not to use one. Then, when she gives you a compliment for something as simple as changing her air conditioning filters, or helping clean out her pantry, or bringing her a Chick-fil-A dinner, or mowing the lawn, or taking her to Pittsburgh to the doctor, that compliment is all the sweeter. People who are in pain very often offer pain to those who can relieve their pain. Yet, in the end, apologies, compliments, and love comes forth, and we are more excellent because of it.

Ann was in pain. I've never known Ann Cloonan apart from pain. When I started milling around the Cloonans' Pleasant Hills' home, there was a fourteen-year-old girl caring for a grandmother suffering from breast cancer and Alzheimer's, another grandmother who had just had her leg amputated and was battling cancer, a father who had just had a massive heart attack and had lost much of the use of his heart, and a mother who had just had a mastectomy and was battling breast cancer. After that, Ann contracted an autoimmune virus that resulted in stage-four cirrhosis of the liver, and she developed pulmonary fibrosis, a condition from which there is no cure. Eighteen years ago, the love of her life passed away within a month of finding out he had brain cancer. On top of all that, Ann's father tragically passed away when she was only twelve years old. I understand everyone has a story, and I understand that tragedy is a part of every individual's life. Still, Ann's life resembles Job's. Dear friends, Lesley and I tried very hard to offer the Gospel to

Ann over the years. Maybe sometimes we acted more as Bildad, Eliphaz, and Zophar keeping Ann from God rather than drawing her towards. Yet we just kept trying to be kind. We just kept offering the Gospel. Lesley chose to serve rather than be served and gave her heart to her mother as a ransom. Honestly, I just tried to take a few steps back, trim the hedges once a year, and mow the lawn once a week. We didn't preach. We just loved. Dalice came by. Lucy came by. Deb came by. The boys showed Grandma the face of Christ. The people from the Lutheran Church kept bringing Holy Communion. One planted. One watered. Ultimately, God provided the increase. Ann died peacefully in her sleep with her Bible by her side. Everything she lost was restored … and even better. She has peace with her neighbor and peace with God.

Her peace with God came as she loved those who were the closest to her.

Ann loved Forrest Cloonan. I've told many a person, including my own boys, there is someone out there for everyone. Ann and her friend Midge needed a ride to a football game in Virginia one night; Forrest Cloonan, ten years the girls' senior, had a car and enjoyed football. Midge asked Forrest to drive them to the game. Forrest agreed, and not long after, Forrest Cloonan and Ann Hilleary eloped. They left the state and came back. They raised a little girl who is beautiful inside and out, and they made her a lady. They gave her away to a boy who was taller than her and who made her laugh. He promised to love her and care for her. He's done his best. Their daughter blessed them with three grandsons, and the two who started with a ride to a football game have loved one another through marriage, parenthood, grandparenthood, death, eighteen years of longing, and now eternal life. A million years from now, because of Christ, Ann will still be loving Forrest.

Ann Cloonan was the greatest grandma. She's been keeping our boys every Friday night since the boys were born. We had a handful of bumps in the road, and there were certainly times when Les and I were more committed to having the boys be with us than be with Ann, but for Tanner, Garrett, and Cameron, being with Ann is one of the best things we could have ever done for our children. Ann was a phenomenal grand-mother. She fed our kids stuff for breakfast no child should ever eat. Pepsi and ice cream is not the breakfast of champions, but it does create a loving bond between a grandmother and her boys. She championed their ball games, their concerts, their field shows, their academic accomplishments and their work in the community, and she never failed to tell them how their granddad certainly would be proud. Ann loved the boys. It is love for her little boys that makes Ann a great grandmother.

Then there is Lesley. My lovely wife told me I was not to say much about her in this eulogy, but it is my responsibility to say something. From the moment Ann purchased a microwave in the early eighties so Lesley wouldn't burn her hair on the burners of the stovetop while she was cooking for the sick family members staying at the Cloonan household, it is easy to see Ann's love and care for her daughter. Ann was tough on Lisa Gresko, Steve Davis, Coach Shepherd, and Don Husted, but she simply wanted the best for her daughter. Ann was Lesley's biggest fan. Ann and Forrest traversed the country with Lesley teaching her, loving her, and showing her off to the world. Lesley Cloonan stands as Forrest and Ann's greatest work of art. To them, Lesley was greater than any quilt, any tole painting, any song played on a Presbyterian pipe organ. To Forrest and Ann, Lesley was more beautiful than any grandeur this state holds. They wanted the world to see her beauty. I believe, though, what made Ann love Lesley the most is the fact that she took what she learned as a twelve-year-old girl caring for the sick in their home and made it her life's work. For thirty-five years, Ann has proudly watched her daughter make basket upon basket, create beautiful art, establish a strong home and place in the community, and change a community for Jesus Christ. But, above all, I believe Ann loves Lesley the most because she has raised a daughter who is committed to seeing that the lame walk, the blind see, the sick are visited, and those who are lonely know they have someone who will love them. It's a daughter's love that has made a mother most proud. And that daughter's love changed a mother-in-law and a son-in-law, too.

Eighteen years ago this Christmas, Ann was in a very dark place. It was the week between Christmas and New Year. Lesley and I went up to Ann's and what happened was not good. Forrest had been gone for less than a year and Ann was hurting. When we got there the situation was volatile to say the least. In the midst of it all and in her grief, Ann began to strike me over and over with both hands on my chest. I was less than cordial at that time, but for whatever reason I chose not to react. As the fists stopped the tears rolled, and silence filled the room, Lesley looked at her mom and said, "Mom, there's nothing you will ever do to Kevin that's going to make him stop loving you." As I look back on those words now, I know to that point I hadn't ever offered Ann the love of Christ. I couldn't stop loving Ann, because I hadn't truly started. Yet, in that moment, day by day, week by week, month by month, year by year, for nearly two decades Ann and I began offering one another the love of Christ. Jesus says, "Love those who hate you. Bless those who curse you. Pray for those who spitefully use you." Ann and I did that. On the days I hated her, she loved me. And on the days she cursed me, I blessed her. And, over time, the example Lesley set for both of us broke down the walls of a mother who didn't want to lose her daughter, and of a husband who wasn't willing to share. In recent years, as I stood at Ann's front door covered with grass and sweat, drinking the bottle of water Ann always had waiting for me, Ann would … occasionally … tell me, "I love you, Kevin." And, with that cool cup of water provided for the prophet by his mother-in-law, I would say, "I love you too, Ann."

And we both meant it.

Dear friends, Ann Cloonan is one of the richest people I have ever known, and we will miss her very much.

May the peace of God that rests upon Ann rest upon each of you this day.

CHAPTER II

HOPE FOR ONE ADDICTED TO HEROIN

I met Steven Brown roughly two years prior to his overdose. Our local assembly is a house of worship famous for welcoming ruffians. Steven Brown was raised as a country kid who turned into an insurance salesman, who turned into a ruffian. By the time I met Steve, he was a man in his fifties who was no longer working in the family insurance business. By the time I met Steve he was a biker who was working in the oil and gas fields. He was a fracker, and biker, and I would soon find out, a heroin addict. Like so many others in our country, Steve was becoming an opioid statistic as he attempted to overmedicate his physical and emotional pain away.

When Steve got to me, he had two little girls and a marriage on life support. How he found our church I do not know, but he did. I spoke with him. I spoke with his wife. I spoke to them both. Steve used the granddaddy of all curse words far too much, but I knew the closer he got to Christ the more that would take care of itself. In time it did. Soon the four Browns were all in church Sunday after Sunday. I remember a Good Friday service in particular just watching Steve and his wife sitting together in our sanctuary worshipping and praying without a word, but even without words there was more than enough love between them. Not long after, in another meeting in my office, Steve surrendered his life to Jesus and His reconciling Gospel.

Jesus teaches, both then and now, "The thief comes only to steal and kill and destroy; I came that they may have life, and have it abundantly." (John 10:10 NASB) Just because a man has surrendered his life to the abundant life of Christ does not mean the thief will stop trying to steal, kill, and destroy. On the night before Steve was scheduled to go to rehab, his family was stolen from. Steve chose to take one last hit of the enemy's killing agent. Yet the reconciliation provided by Christ and Steve's submission to it saw to it that Steven Brown is not eternally destroyed.

Until the time of his passing, Steve had been estranged from much of his family. On the night of Steve's funeral visitation at our church, it was my honor to tell Steve's dad that his son had given his life to Christ. Amidst the deafening sorrow, Steve's dad cried in relief.

Certainly some among my evangelical family will call me a fool for saying so, but they know all too well even guilty, dying thieves with no hope for a stay of execution most assuredly join the crucified and innocent Savior in Paradise.

We buried Steve right before Christmas.

The eulogy of Steven Brown

I nearly never read obituaries during funeral services. Much of the time I find them to be impersonal and not even touching the depth of the deceased life. Yet, Steve's is rich and filled with people, and places, and activities I never knew about Steve.

Allow me to read Steve's obituary, and then I will explain further.

Steven Michael Brown, fifty-four, was the son of Steven E. Brown of Kaneswood and the late C. C. Brown of Ronaldsburg. In addition to his father he is survived by his loving wife, Diann (Yates) Brown whom he married October 4, 2002, in Moab, Utah; two precious daughters, Meredith Brown and Angelina Brown; sister Susan Grazier and husband Larry Grazier; brother Ralph Brown and wife, Cadence; niece Carly Grazier; nephews Bill Grazier and Lance Brown; mother- and father-in-law Jack and Mary Yates; brother-in-law Edwin Yates and wife Paulette; uncles and aunts; cousins; and many many friends.

Steve was born in Morgantown on May 2,1962. He graduated from Central High School in 1980. Following high school, Steve attended WVU graduating with a Bachelor of Science in Business. Steve spent most of his career cooperating Brown Insurance Agency along with his father and brother. Following an early retirement, he stepped outside of his comfort zone to pursue an interest in the oil and gas industry working as a pipeline inspector for the past four years.

Steve loved life! He was a true adventure seeker and risk taker in every way, loving to have fun. He was a free spirit who loved spending time involving the outdoors. Steve could water-ski barefoot, snow-skied the Rocky Mountains, kayaked class 5 and 6 rivers, had his pilot's license and flew his own plane. He loved to go hunting, fishing, camping, and hiking. He took a family vacation rock crawling along the Rubicon Trail in California and traveled thousands of miles cross country riding his Harley with friends. He also enjoyed many wonderful trips with family and friends to Mexico, Costa Rica, Canada, and all over the United States.

Currently Steve attended the Kingdom Evangelical Methodist Church in Westover. He had a gracious heart and was always willing to help out anyone in need. He never met a stranger and treated everyone he met equally. Above all, Steve was a devoted husband and loving father. He loved spending time with his family, he taught Meredith how to ride a dirt bike and to shoot a bow. He enjoyed taking Angelina to local parks and playgrounds and taught her how to swim. He would do anything to see a smile and truly enjoyed spending time with "his girls."

Dear friends, the Steve I knew only existed in a handful of sentences and the final paragraph of this obituary. I did not know Steve for the first fifty-two-and-a-half years of his life. I only knew him for the last year-and-a-half. From that context I am not fool enough to try to tell any of you how Steve lived his life. Your stories of Steve are your stories, and you should spend the rest of your days allowing your memories of him to define you.

We are truly defined by those whom we have lost.

I am imagining that perhaps the Steve I knew is a bit different from the Steve you knew. I'm not saying that Steve was two-faced, or a phony, or even ashamed of the spiritual transformation he experienced, but what *I am* saying is that I met a Steve who desired a very different life from the one he was coming up against in all his labors, all his travels, all his adventures, and all his experiences. My life with Steven Brown began two years ago when his wife, Diann, began attending Kingdom.

Most of life is panorama, and as I look out at the nearly 800 people who attend Kingdom on a weekly basis, sadly most of the people blend into the panorama rather than draw near to a personal relationship with me and the other pastors. We do our best as our church grows larger to see that it grows smaller, but unless folks make themselves known to us, it is very difficult to get to know them. After about six months, Diann chose to make herself known.

Diann made an appointment with me, and she told me about herself, her kids, and her husband. The courage to be vulnerable is truly the greatest strength, and Diann was very courageous that day. She was honest with me, and I learned about Steve's dreams and his nightmares. It wasn't long after that that Steve began coming to Kingdom, and soon enough he made an appointment to come talk with me.

Folks, I have to be honest with you. While my grandmother's father was a Methodist minister, my dad is a Marine Corps veteran who owned a hydraulic and machine shop. Needless to say, while much of my upbringing was Christian in culture and I made a personal commitment to Jesus of Nazareth as my Lord and Savior at the age of ten, I also like to say: I do not have virgin ears or eyes. Both of those facts seemed to bring Steve much comfort that day we were speaking for the very first time. Steve could be himself with me. I didn't judge him. I just tried to listen to his story.

I learned quickly that Steve was a man with calloused hands, and calloused days, but not a heart so calloused that the seed of God's Word couldn't get in. We talked for over an hour that day. I shared the Gospel with Steve, and he told me he would think about it. I didn't try to coerce him into a relationship with Christ. I could have, I thought. I was a salesman in the nasty hydraulics industry before I was a preacher. Yet, in the hour I knew Steve, I had too much respect for him to try to pull a fast one on him like many preachers who desire notches in their gun belts rather than genuine relationship so often do.

I walked Steve to the door. He told me he would think about the Gospel. We shook calloused hands. Steve drove off but not into the sunset.

Steven Brown came back to Sunday worship with Diann, Meredith, and Angelina. Week after week, Sunday after Sunday, there sat Steve genuine among the panorama. Then he made another appointment, and another. Steve cried in my office. Steve cursed in my office. Steve always had the respect to apologize.

You see, friends, Jesus once was asked by a lawyer who was trying to trick Him that if a person could keep one rule in all of life, what rule should be kept? Jesus told that ol' lawyer that the one thing is actually two things. Jesus said if we're going to get this life right, we have to properly balance love of God and love of neighbor. Here's the problem: Most folks either spend so much time loving God that they fail to love their neighbor; which means they're not really loving God at all—and, other folks spend so much time loving neighbor that they don't actually ever take the time to really ever find out what it means to love God. Both types of folks are equally lost and equally separated from God and the people God has put around them. I believe Steve was on to this little riddle of life, and that is why he was running so hard. You knew him better than I did, but it is easy to see from the pictures that Steve spent much of his life loving and living big, but, like there is in all of us, Steve knew that there was something still missing.

So, with that in mind, Steve and I just kept meeting. We talked and talked. He was brutally honest with me about everything he was coming against and with everything that was coming against him. And then one day, Steve and Diann were sitting on my couch. They were sitting on the same cushion.

Most couples who sit on my couch sit on opposite ends of the couch and not on the same cushion. Steve and Diann were sitting on the same cushion.

If I am going to be totally honest with you, I'm not sure either one of them could quote me any part of the Bible in any sort of extended detail. I'm not sure either one of them could quote me the second verse of either "Amazing Grace" or "How Great Thou Art." But thank our God above and among us that He doesn't judge us on Scriptural or hymnal proficiency. We are judged on the Gospel's merits, the Gospel's sufficiency, and our willingness to surrender to it by faith in its beautiful, free grace. This was many months after my initial meeting with Steve. This was many months after Steve had started attending Kingdom with Diann and the girls. This was after many sermons and many brutally honest conversations. Yet there with Steve and Diann sitting on the same couch cushion I asked them both: "Do you acknowledge your individual sins?" To that they both said, "Yes." I asked them both: "Do you acknowledge that God is holy and that our sin separates us from the Holy God?" To that they both said, "Yes." I asked them both: "Do you believe that the only thing that bridges the gap between humanity's death and God's Life is the death, burial, and resurrection of Jesus of Nazareth?" To that they both said, "Yes." Then, with both Steve and Diann sitting on the same couch cushion, I looked at them, now with the most genuine of loves either of them had ever experienced or shared, and with tears streaming down their cheeks, I asked both of them: "Will you surrender your life to Christ's cleansing?" They both said, "Yes." In that moment Steve and Diann became children of the King and my brother and sister in Christ.

Here's how the apostle John describes what Steve and Diann experienced in that moment: "There was the true Light which, coming into the world, enlightens every man. He was in the world, and the world was made through Him, and the world did not know Him. He came to His own, and those who were His own did not receive Him. But as many as received Him, to them He gave the right to become children of God, even to those who believe in His name, who were born, not of blood nor of the will of the flesh nor of the will of man, but of God." (John 1:9–13 NASB)

That day in my office, both Steve and Diann were born. They were born not of blood, nor of the will of the flesh, nor of the will of man, but of God. For fifty-two-and-a-half years, Steven Brown did his very best at seeking life and love. Often Steve did a fine job loving neighbor apart from loving God and, I imagine while apart from every neighbor in the world while riding his Harley or climbing the Rocky Mountains, or shooting the rapids on the New, Gauley, or Cheat Rivers, Steve spoke to God trying with all his humanity to love the God Who created him. Yet it wasn't until months ago that the two came together. That day Steve surrendered to Christ, and he began loving God and neighbor at the exact same time.

Even when we have surrendered to Christ, we are not immune from the arrows of the enemy. Jesus Himself warns that once a house has been swept clean, the enemy will leave for a season and then return with reinforcements. Jesus teaches that surrender to Him and life more abundant does not eliminate the enemy's desire to steal, kill, and destroy. Yet I also know that no matter how hard the enemy strikes, Paul's words to the Church at Rome can never die:

"Who will separate us from the love of Christ? Will tribulation, or distress, or persecution, or famine, or nakedness, or peril, or sword? Just as it is written,

"FOR YOUR SAKE WE ARE BEING PUT TO DEATH ALL DAY LONG; WE WERE CONSIDERED AS SHEEP TO BE SLAUGHTERED." But in all these things we overwhelmingly conquer through Him who loved us. For I am convinced that neither death, nor life, nor angels, nor principalities, nor things present, nor things to come, nor powers, nor height, nor depth, nor any other created thing, will be able to separate us from the love of God, which is in Christ Jesus our Lord."

(ROMANS 8:35–39 NASB)

Steve may be separated from his brothers and sisters in Christ temporarily, but Steven Brown is not separated from the love and presence of the one true God. I know nothing of Steve's first fifty-two-and-a-half years, but what I know of Steven Brown's last year-and-a-half is a surrender to Life Himself. Steve gave his life to Christ. Diann has given her life to Christ. I stood in the lake this past summer as Meredith was baptized declaring her submission to Christ. And I have no doubt that one day when Angelina is faced with the decision to receive Christ as her Savior, she too will surrender to Jesus of Nazareth. This family will stand with their Lord and one another for all eternity. I pray that each of you surrender and receive the same, that you love God and neighbor, that you receive eternal life even as Steve did.

Let not your hearts be troubled, and neither be afraid....

May the peace and blessing of our God that rests upon Steve rest upon each of you this evening.

CHAPTER III

DUPLEXES AND D-DAY:
A LOVE STORY

Tom Brokaw writes:

"When the United States entered World War II, the US government turned to ordinary Americans and asked of them extraordinary service, sacrifice, and heroics. Many Americans met those high expectations, and then returned home to lead ordinary lives.

When the war ended, more than twelve million men and women put their uniforms aside and returned to civilian life. They went back to work at their old jobs or started small businesses; they became big-city cops and firemen; they finished their degrees or enrolled in college for the first time; they became schoolteachers, insurance salesmen, craftsmen, and local politicians. They weren't widely known outside their families or their communities. For many, the war years were enough adventure to last a lifetime. They were proud of what they accomplished but they rarely discussed their experiences, even with each other. They became once again ordinary people, the kind of men and women who always have been the foundation of the American way of life." (Tom Brokaw, *The Greatest Generation*, pg. 14)

I never met Foster Feathers. His daughter taught school with my mother, his banker son-in-law loaned my church the money to purchase our church property, and one of his grandsons is my wife's dentist. At Foster's passing, the family needed a preacher. They knew of me. I knew of them. They asked the funeral director to ask me. I was available.

I'm glad I was.

*Just like every family for whom I officiate funerals, I asked Mr. Feathers family my tried-and-true statement, which is, "I don't want any of you walking out of here tomorrow saying, 'I wish Kevin would have said, **this.**' You tell me the, **this** and I'll put it all together for you."*

There were many remembrances that followed, but the love story they told me of Foster and his wife of seventy-four years, Elizabeth, is the greatest love story I have ever been told.

The two were kids living in separate sides of the same duplex. Foster was older. Elizabeth was younger. Their ages were close and the families were friendly, but the boy and the girl were just a little too distant in age to date, so the families forbade it. Somehow, Foster and Elizabeth had to find a way.

Each night at an appointed time, both Foster and Elizabeth would ascend the stairs of their respective sides of their duplex. They would go into their respective bathrooms. They would turn on the water of their respective sinks and lower their voices. Then, face to face, with two-by-fours, plaster, and wallpaper separating them, the two lovebirds would talk every night unbeknownst to their parents. It went on like this for years, until Foster and his brothers joined the service prior to the D-Day invasions.

There would be no more conversations through bathroom walls. Foster went to basic training and then to the European theater of World War II. Foster and Elizabeth began writing letters to one another. There were letters written by one, or the other, or both every day.

As Elizabeth sat in her wheelchair as the family relayed these stories and memories to me, the new widow said nothing. I said to them all, "There must have been thousands of letters." I looked at silent Elizabeth and said, "Do you still have all the letters?"

She nodded once.

Foster and Elizabeth, two ordinary people who always have been the foundation of the American way of life.

The eulogy of Foster Feathers

Tomorrow morning I will begin my sermon with these words from Micah the prophet:

"He has told you, O man, what is good;
And what does the Lord require of you
But to do justice, to love kindness,
And to walk humbly with your God?"

(MICAH 6:8 NASB)

I begin with this Scripture tomorrow because it has been my experience that folks make Christianity more complicated than what it is, or they minimize it to a simple ideology void of the standards of holiness. Christianity is simple but never simpler. Simply stated, it is loving our Creator through faith in Jesus' Gospel, and loving with heart, soul, mind, and strength those whom the Lord has placed within our spheres of influence. That is Christianity ... no more, no less. Love God. Love neighbor. Act justly. Love mercy. Walk humbly with your God.

I've never had a conversation with Foster Feathers. I never even knew him. Yes, Foster's daughter taught school with my mother. Foster's son-in-law loaned our local church the money to purchase our present church property. Foster's grandson is my wife's dentist. Still, I never knew Foster Feathers nor his religious convictions. Yet I do know that the Scriptures teach that we will be known by the spiritual fruit that in our lives is evident. As a pastor in these situations I certainly memorialize, but I also look for fruit. I can tell you not only is there plenty to memorialize about Foster Feathers, there is also a great deal of spiritual fruit on the vine.

I have every intention of speaking of Foster and Elizabeth's marriage, Foster's commitment to an honest day's work, his patriotism, and his quiet faith, but first I'd like to speak of the dashes of salt and breaks of light from Foster's life that brought flavor and vibrancy to you all.

Out of the shoot yesterday, I heard that Foster had a nickname for everyone. If you were Foster's blood, then you received a nickname immediately. If you married in or simply hung around the Feathers' home or world on a consistent basis, a nickname had to be earned. I'm told that I would have had to earn a nickname, and my nickname would have most likely had to do with my height. I'm guessing Foster would not have called me "Slim." Regardless of what he would have called me, those names were terms of endearment for each of you. That's why Dad Dad gave names to his grandchildren, and Fuzzy gave names to each of his coworkers at Sterling Faucet all those years. He loved you, and you had Foster's trust and his heart.

Foster's joy brought joy to each of you. The massive joke book that he kept close to his side was studied over and again. You know that every conversation with Foster ended with three or four jokes. Foster remembered the jokes word for word, but not that he had told you the same jokes many times before … or maybe he did, and now the joke is on each of you. Regardless, as the old veteran stood under the American Flag he daily appropriately raised at dawn, lowered at dusk, and took down in the elements, he always stood waving to you as you headed to your car and back to your world.

The joy and pride of Foster's life was always ringing in your hearts and singing loudly in your ears. Foster Feathers was not only a jokester, he was also a crooner and sometimes even a rocker. Someone said yesterday, "He could siiiiiiiiiiing." Foster loved Glen Miller, loved the Rat Pack, and on occasion could be found jamming in the basement of his home with his own band, Dad Dad & the Rockers. Despite Bruce Springsteen's claims of ownership, it was Dad Dad & the Rockers whose greatest hit was "Born in the USA."

You can see Foster Feathers was a very rich man. His riches were housed in Sycamore Lanes as he bowled with his friends for over forty years. Foster's riches were stored in backyard summers where he and his family would engage in epic badminton matches. His treasures were found in Neapolitan ice cream, popcorn, Faygo pop, and a Miller High Life every day at three o'clock. Foster Feathers' treasure was before the world to see in a ninetieth birthday party at Gene's over a dog, a beer, and hair that was never out of place. The world may not have believed his age, but Foster Feathers' treasures of ninety-three years were easy to see.

Foster's love was his treasure. He and Elizabeth are treasures. Seventy-four years together. The Bible promises that life is to be seen as three score and ten, but Foster and Elizabeth exceeded the lifespan with a marriage that lasted seventy years. What began as kids in a duplex, with a bathroom wall between them, grew to daily letters through WWII, and finally a marriage that stands as a testimony to us all. This is the greatness of Foster Feathers.

He and Elizabeth stand as part of the greatest generation ever. Foster was a WWII Purple Heart veteran serving in the Army 359th Engineer Corps. He was part of the Allied Invasion on Omaha Beach on June 8, 1944, D-Day Plus Two... his twenty-first birthday. Foster is among the most courageous in our history.

Foster carried that courage back home in a rucksack of commonality. Foster served each of us by helping us overcome tyranny, and then he just went back to work. Forty-plus years at Sterling Faucet as a foundry supervisor, Foster worked afternoon shift every single day. His dedication to excellence was alive there but was just as noticeable in the

90-degree angle of his hedges, the straight lines in his yard, and in the proficiency with which a home is to be painted.

Yet perhaps Foster's greatest evidence of his faith and spiritual fruitfulness is to be seen in his commitment to daily private prayer before he headed to bed.

You see, friends, Foster Feathers did the two things God calls each of us to do in order to find His favor: love God and love neighbor. No more, no less…Act justly. Love mercy. Walk humbly with your God. This is the life of Foster Feathers, and it is a life to which we should all aspire

May the peace and blessing of our God rest upon Foster and each of you this day.

CHAPTER IV

WHO IS MY MOTHER?

As a kid growing up, L.J. was never L.J. Instead, L.J. was Larry. He was in my older sister's class two years my senior. His parents knew my parents. My family knew his family. His younger brother was in my class. After his high school graduation, I lost track of Larry. He must have become L.J. during that time.

Amy was a girl who was also my age. I honestly do not remember if she went to high school at Morgantown High School or the competing high school, University High. It doesn't matter. We all knew one another, and in some form or another, we were all friends. After our high school graduation year of 1988, I lost track of Amy too.

Jane is a woman I met in September of 1993. I had just turned twenty-three and for my birthday, my parents gave me and my little-more-than-a-year bride a piece of property to build a home. Jane was the loan officer at the bank who handled our first mortgage. We have banked with Jane ever since.

God's tapestries are the most intricate.

L.J. married Amy.

Jane married Jeff.

Simultaneously alongside with these, but with the three barely touching, Lesley and I were living our life with the other two couples.

Jane and Jeff were members of our church for a short period of time, but as lives often do, the two saw their church attendance growing less and less. I still saw Jane at the bank, and we remained friends. She and Jeff divorced.

L.J. and Amy were married. I wasn't invited to the wedding, but I had no reason to be. I was no more in L.J. and Amy's sphere of influence than they were in mine. They were living happily ever after with career, house, and family pictures holding now their two daughters and son: Lizzy, Reagan, and Cooper. Some time as the twentieth century faded into the twenty-first, Amy was diagnosed with cancer. She died in 2005. Lizzy was eight. Reagan was six. Cooper was two. L.J. was now a single father and a widower.

L.J. was in real estate.

Jane was in banking.

After L.J.'s grief had subsided, the two had dinner and then a date.

They were married nearly two years after Amy had passed.

They asked me to do their wedding on New Year's Eve, 2006.

Nearly three years later, Jane officially adopted Lizzy, Reagan, and Cooper. While Amy's memory would never fade, the kids lovingly began to call Jane "Mom."

As before, I would see Jane at the bank and L.J. about town, but the new family was attending church services at a different church on the other side of town much nearer to their home. Pastors should never view another church as competition— though many do. Personally, I was excited they were attending. From the distant outside, it appeared to me that all was going very well within the new L.J. and Jane Haines' household.

Then, in the late summer of 2013, Jane showed up on my schedule. She arrived at my office for her scheduled appointment, but I had no inkling as to why she was seeing me at my office rather than me seeing her at my bank. She sat down, began to cry, and told me she and L.J. were in a very bad place. Like nearly every other marriage is at some point their marriage was crumbling, and we were meeting to come up with an estimate and decide whether fixing the marriage was worth the cost of repairs. Jane believed it was, so I reached out to L.J.

With our relationship being characterized as more of a childhood acquaintance than a friendship, L.J. and I had never spoken to one another in this manner before. He was very candid with me and agreed to do whatever he needed to in order to repair his marriage. I sent him home that day with Alex and Stephen Kendrick's book, The Love Dare. L.J. was committed to doing everything necessary to win the heart of his wife.

I would like to say the repairs began slowly, but they didn't. L.J. was all in. From late summer into early autumn, he was actively engaging in The Love Dare's daily assignments for repairing a marriage, and soon the family of five began weekly attending my local church. Week after week L.J. and I were meeting, and the love between L.J. and Jane was being rekindled.

Then mid-autumn, L.J. came down with pneumonia. Ultimately he was hospitalized with a severe strain of the pulmonary illness. Over a period of weeks, L.J. overcame and returned to our weekly meetings and worship services, but then late one Saturday night I received a call from Jane. L.J. was sick again, and the two were heading to our local hospital's emergency room. L.J. was worse, and this time he had to be life-flighted to the University of Pittsburgh Medical Center, one hour north of us in Pittsburgh, Pennsylvania.

October turned into November, and November turned into Christmas. There were days where L.J. was recovering. There were days when setbacks arose. Then on New Year's Eve of 2013, after months of being in the hospital, a girlfriend of Jane's called me from Pittsburgh.

"Kevin," she said, "Jane would like you to come to the hospital. They don't think L.J. is going to make it."

I visited a couple days later.

There is no sense in describing the intensive care unit scene. It is one all of us can imagine objectively amidst our own subjective experiences.

We held L.J.'s hands. We sat silently. We looked at all the cards and pictures hanging on his walls. Though L.J. and I had discussed his relationship with Christ, I whispered the Gospel into the ears of his medically-induced coma once again. We prayed.

Just weeks later, on February 8, 2014, I eulogized L.J., my childhood acquaintance and adulthood brother-in-Christ, as L.J.'s three children and their mother looked on.

While Jesus commands us to call no man father, the Messiah would never deny the man who loved Him as his Son. It was most likely Gabriel who said to Joseph, "Joseph, son of David, do not be afraid to take Mary as your wife; for the Child who has been conceived in her is of the Holy Spirit. She will bear a Son; and you shall call His name Jesus, for He will save His people from their sins." (Matthew 1:20, 21 NASB) Joseph took a Child void of his heredity as his own. He cared for Him as the gift of God He was and remains to be. It is recorded in the same Gospel of Matthew that more than thirty years after this angelic visitation, the Son Joseph raised as his own, when told His mother was waiting for Him outside, spoke these words of true motherhood, saying, "Who is my mother...? For whoever does the will of My Father who is in heaven, he is My brother and sister and mother." (Matthew 12:48, 50 NASB)

What is required to be the mother of three children?

All that is required for motherhood is the sacrificial love of Christ that longs to do the will of the Father in heaven.

The eulogy of LJ Haines

Frame of reference is an extremely powerful component within all of life's circumstances. One person sees something one way, and another individual sees it from his perspective. Typically, it is frame of reference that stands as the great divider of community rather than the complimentary harmonizer. In nearly all cases you and I want the sole vision to be your and my individual vision. I see it my way. You see it yours. A genteel smile is offered, but both walk away believing he is correct. Very rarely in our society do we find consensus. Yet, it was consensus that was found when I asked LJ's family to tell me his gift.

Whether it was Jane, Lizzy, Reagan, Cooper, or other family members, each of them, within their individual frames of reference, offered a harmonious explanation of LJ's gift to each of us. Be it from a wife's frame of reference, or a child's, a father's, or a mother's, a brother or a sister, the song that was sung of LJ's character was consistent. For the last three days, this is the song that has been sung to me. It is a song not from my voice but from the hearts who love LJ the most. The chorus sung goes a little something like this:

I wasn't looking for someone. I was looking for peace, strength, genuine love, and stability. When I met LJ, I felt like my prayers had been answered. It was so strange ... LJ and I had so many of the same friends over the years, but our paths never crossed. LJ always had so much energy and fun. He was what every woman wanted: he may not have enjoyed shopping, but he possessed a willingness to make me happy. He was the kind of man who would send clothes back to the boutique dressing room, telling the saleswoman, "Tell her to try this on. It will look amazing on her."

Relationships are always so uncertain, but LJ told me it was after a simple Saturday afternoon of mulching the lawn that he knew we were to be together forever. There were lots of chance encounters, but God's timing is always perfect. Someone once told us, "Yours has always been my favorite love story."

I love him because LJ is a dreamer. He dreamed about buildings and projects ... and hot dog shops. Still after all the dreaming, it was a commitment to simplicity where we found ourselves. He wanted to walk away from the business world. LJ wanted to help people. He told me he wanted to be a counselor. He had coached so many young businesspeople to the place where they were experiencing success. Still, LJ wanted to go deeper. He wanted to grow their hearts and not simply a portfolio.

After all of these, I have something so special to cling to. I found something LJ wrote this past fall. It simply read, "I just want to greet Jane with a smile and a kiss every day."

LJ was a brother and a son to all, even those who were outside his own bloodlines. He touched the hearts of everyone.

Even his own doctor cried.

I do not know of a greater husband, a greater father, a greater son, a greater brother, a greater uncle, a greater friend.

Our brother was fun-loving and charismatic. He always spoke for me, and before any and everything I ever did, I wanted to speak to LJ first. I even approached LJ before I proposed to my wife.

LJ has lived as our advice giver, our care giver; he took care of all of us.

He was the most sensitive man I have ever known. I think he even cried at Hallmark commercials. Certainly I forgive him for babysitting me by placing me on a dugout at the park as he ran off to hang with his friends. Why wouldn't I?

Our brother lived as absorption. He lived as our buffer to the struggles of this world. It was LJ who took care of things.

He always spoke for me, so now it's time for me to speak for him. We loved golfing with Dad. The betting, the jokes, the smack talk, the bets as to when Dad would hurl his first club in anger—we loved it all.

Larry would always call and just say, "Hey, Sis. Just wanted to check in." He hated long phone conversations but never failed to check in. My children love their uncle Smell Jay. He followed them on Instagram, played with his nieces and nephews, and even made balloon animals. Who knows how to make balloon animals?!?! Our kids absolutely love Morgantown, and it is because of their uncle LJ. Family truly mattered to him.

Our brother was the greatest of dreamers who, with projects scattered about, seemed to never finish a thing he started. But the one thing LJ always completed was the wrapping of his arms around us. Our brother always possessed open arms.

I will miss his love for old movies.

I will miss his counsel.

We will miss LJ's smile.

Our dad was funny. He was outgoing. There was always a smile on his face.

He was a great dancer.

He was nice. That's a good thing to say, isn't it? Our dad was nice.

We love the fact that when our dad watched <u>Extreme Home Makeover</u> and Ty Pennington said, "Bus driver, move that bus!" our dad would always cry.

Our dad was an excellent cook. He made the best chicken stir fry and the best burgers.

He loved bad eighties music (you know there's only about thirty good songs from the eighties) and he loved the Mountaineers, the Steelers, the Primanti Brothers' sandwiches, and the corners of brownies.

But, more than anything, he loved us.

I remember my son's smile and how I looked forward to seeing that smile every single day across from me at our booth at IHOP.

My son loved the first snow of the year. I don't mean the first flurries, but the first significant snow of the year. From the time LJ was sixteen, when the snow began to measurably fall, we would go to Ruby & Ketchy's for breakfast, and then we would drive deep into Preston County. We would drive and drive until we would get hung up. I really don't remember where we would end up each time, but I do remember the conversation between us. It was great conversation.

We loved to golf. It was always competitive, with plenty of psychological warfare going on. There were bets on score, tee shots, closest to the pin, and my sons would always seem to have a bet on when I would blow up or send a golf club through the side of my leg. And there was always a foursome. I guess we're looking for a fourth now. Whoever was chosen as scorekeeper, he couldn't know how to keep score, because my son was a terrible scorekeeper. The new fourth has to have a twenty handicap but play to a ten, just like LJ. More than anything, the new fourth has to make everyone laugh.

I guess there will never be a new fourth who could ever measure up to our fourth who was always first.

You see, our fourth lit up a room. Our fourth possessed an immeasurable kindness. Our fourth was always polite ... mannerly ... and respectful. Our fourth was the picture of the Beatitudes. Read the fifth chapter of the Gospel of Matthew and you'll see my son. He only spoke words that built people up. His gift? My son's gift was his ability and commitment to treat CEOs and ditch diggers the exact same way.

You can look at me and say you have done well in raising your son, but one thing is for certain: it is my son who has done well. He did well.

LJ loved our home. He would say time and again, "Mom, when are you going to sell me this place?" When we would leave for an RV excursion, my son would help himself to our house. He wouldn't ask. He didn't need to. He wouldn't tell us. He didn't need to. We could tell ... all the potato chips were gone.

It's an honor to say that my son's personality was his gift. He was a leader, a typical firstborn. He lived a life of watching after me, his mother. LJ, my son, was a wonderful family man. It was always family, always friends, with him.

My son saw to it that there was always a volleyball net in the backyard. Everyone seemed to gather around him. He always turned everything into fun.

As LJ's mom, I was always honored and humbled that he would send me flowers on his birthday.

He is the greatest example ... always.

This is the same song I heard sung from ten different frames of reference. Some sang a soprano ... some sang bass ... some sang with a soothing quietness ... some sang with a measured loudness. Regardless, all sang the same song of LJ's gift. The beautiful reality of LJ's life-song sang by his family is not that each, independently of one another, offered up the same lyrics. The glory of the song is that LJ's life formed their independence into one unified chorus.

LJ's life brought joy into your own. You no longer saw yourself as the world saw you. You saw the light God has made you to be, and with LJ's encouragement, you wanted to let your light so shine before this world. LJ's life taught the whole world to sing in perfect harmony. And now even in his passing he has gathered us around, not himself or this moment, but the things that he stood for: humility, hurting for others, supreme self-control, a hunger and thirst for what is right, mercy, purity of heart, peace, and perseverance. That's the gift of LJ Haines: He didn't want any of us to rally around him: he wanted to simply call us to join with one another around the few things that are right and true. When he came to my office last fall to talk, the two of us spoke of simplicity, truth, and love. The great shedder of tears walked from my office into a new hope and called me to press on with him.

We may all spend our days singing the song of LJ, but I honestly believe this human gift given to each of us calls us to lift our voices and sing of beautiful life rather than simply the man who possessed it. LJ's life calls us to be defined by this one we have lost. His life has unified many; now, with the vibrancy and savor LJ has placed in our hearts, we must live our lives bringing people into the same unity.

May the peace and blessing of our God rest upon LJ and each of us this day.

CHAPTER V

MURDER OF A GOOD BOY

Chuck Sandy went to work that morning just as he had every other morning. He was a hardworking man who owned a towing company in Westover, West Virginia, called Chuck's Towing. He was washing his tow trucks that morning when a competing tow truck company owner walked into his truck bays, sneaked up behind him, and shot him, killing Chuck instantly. Immediately our little town went on alert and lockdown as speculation and the manhunt for Chuck Sandy's murderer began. Later that evening, the murderer took his own life. The saga ended for most of our town, but for the family it was only beginning.

My name often seems to rise to the surface as the requested preacher when tragedies such as this one occur. While I did not live a rebellious life in any form, my family has always been around the rougher side of our small town. My great-grandfather, grandfather, and father all either worked in or owned machine shops. I worked in my father's machine shop from the age of thirteen to thirty-two. My great-uncle owned a body shop. Alcoholism has been prevalent in my family tree. If my hometown of Morgantown, West Virginia, is known as the University City, then my home place of Westover, West Virginia, is the other side

119

of the tracks west over the Monongahela River. Suffice to say, I understand the difference between holiness and sterility; and I also know quite a few blue-collar folks who, even after washing their hands, eat their food with dirty fingernails.

While I knew a number of people who worked for Chuck Sandy, my neighbor included, I never met Chuck Sandy. Though I knew of him, until I saw his body lying in the casket, I had never set my eyes on him in my life.

The day we buried Chuck was also near Christmas. It was cold and wet. It was one of those days when it was too warm to snow, but the temperature of the rain was chilling. When I got to the funeral home for the funeral, there were tow trucks from every towing company in town. Parked where the hearse is typically parked on the day of funerals waited a flat/tilt-bed tow truck with the hearse loaded up and ready to go.

I walked into the funeral home and questioned the funeral directors, saying, "What am I riding in to the cemetery?"

They laughed and answered, "The hearse."

My eyes grew wide and I said, "You have got to be kidding me?!"

They weren't.

When the funeral concluded—and it was a raucous one—we processed outside in that cold rain with the casket covered. The flatbed was now tilted; the casket was loaded; the funeral director and I hopped up in that hearse; the tow truck driver leveled out the bed and we were on our way.

Never before.

Hopefully, never again.

It was the first time I ever got car-sick on the way to a committal service. It's in all our best interests if I leave out the details.

As I write this, it may seem that I am making light of the tragedy. I am not. Chuck Sandy's eulogy and this introduction to it are written very much like it was reported to me that he lived his life. Chuck worked hard, and he played hard. He did his best during both, and all points in between, to bless the lives of those around him.

During his service, the Zac Brown Band song, "Toes," was played.

You can look up the lyrics if you'd like.

The eulogy of Chuck Sandy

I've only been in this position two other times in my life, and both were equally difficult. I know none of you expected to be here this day under these conditions. Everyone most likely had it in his and her minds that each would be washing trucks, towing cars, and getting ready for a well-deserved weekend. But here we stand. Yesterday I told Carla, Chuck Jr., and Kandy that they have every right to be angry. Frankly, I'd be surprised if they weren't. Still, many many years ago, a man named Job had much of what he loved taken away from him, and as folks tried to make sense of a seemingly senseless situation, Job spoke these words, "Though [God] slay me, I will hope in Him. Nevertheless I will argue my ways before Him. This also will be my salvation, for a godless man may not come before His presence"! (Job 13:15, 16 NASB)

As Chuck's wife and children sat with me in that back room yesterday, I told them situations like this keep us bitter or drive us to be better. I could say many things today, but in order to be better, in order to be defined by this one you have lost, it is Chuck Sandy's greatness upon which you must primarily focus. If we do this, healing will come over time, and, over time, the strength of Chuck Sandy's character will come more alive in each of you than you could ever imagine. So tell me: just what was Chuck Sandy's greatness?

As I said to Carla, Chuck Jr., and Kandy yesterday, "I don't want you walking out of here tomorrow saying, 'I wish Kevin would have said this about Dad,'" from each of their lips sang the exact same song. The first lyrics to the song of Chuck's life sung by those closest to him were,

"Dad was always very loving and caring." Now, in the rough and tumble world of the towing business, some of you may be saying it would be impossible to be loving and caring and own a towing business, but look to what you know to be true. Yesterday I watched person after person flood into this place with tears in their eyes, arms around each other, stories of Chuck coming from your hearts, and all of those things were wrapped in Chuck's Towing T-shirts and sweatshirts. Chuck may have rattled some cages at times, he might have been a bit stern, he may have blocked off the interstate a time or two, but people who love and care the most are the people who have to be the strongest. If you are the one who has had the many entrusted to your care, if you are the one who protects the livelihood and happiness of the many, then you do not have the liberty to be weak. You have to be stronger than the strength of most. Strength is your armor. And still, underneath all that armor is a caring, loving heart that is the fuel for the shielding of others. This is how Chuck Sandy lived his life.

There's a powerful passage of Scripture in the tenth chapter of John's Gospel that records Jesus saying that the enemy comes only to kill, steal, and destroy, but our Lord came that we would have life, and that life would be abundant life. In that passage of Scripture, Jesus says He is the door to the sheepfold, and if anyone is going to try to get to His sheep, then the enemy would have to go through Him first. Now, folks, I never really had the opportunity to ever meet Chuck before, but what I've learned from you is Chuck stood at the door of each of your lives and said, "If you are going to try to get to my loved ones, then you're going to have to go through me first."

That is the life Chuck lived before his wife and children. That is the life Chuck lived before his mother and step-father. That is the life Chuck lived before his sisters. That is the life Chuck lived before his nieces and his nephews, and especially his nephew, Dean. Chuck lovingly and protectively lived as the door to your sheep pen.

Someone said to me yesterday that Chuck would not only see that you had everything you ever needed, but in so many cases, Chuck saw to it that you'd have everything you ever wanted. As I sat and listened yesterday, Chuck's niece told me when she was a kid she suffered from severe asthma. One time she needed her inhaler. Chuck answered the call, but not only did Chuck answer the call by going and getting his niece her inhaler, Chuck got the inhaler and brought the entire volunteer fire department with him. It was what his niece needed. I think the old song would say Chuck's attitude of care was one of "Ain't no mountain high, ain't no valley low." Chuck went the distance to meet your needs.

Another person said that Chuck took a whole passel of his family to Disney World once, and instead of getting basic tickets and staying in value resorts, Chuck put everybody up in the Animal Kingdom Lodge, got every family a suite, and treated everyone to all the Mickey and Minnie fixin's they could handle. I read in the obituary that Chuck was the type of person who when he did something, it was to the fullest. That's how Chuck met your needs and wants ... to the fullest.

Now, I have no firsthand knowledge of this, but apparently Chuck was a bit ornery in his early days. What more could one expect from a young man who was driving a tow truck for Sanford's Towing when he was but the age of sixteen? I even heard rumor that ol' Chuck took on the entire University High School football team on the steps of UHS up on Hawk Hill. Chuck Sandy's exploits were legendary. Yet orneriness was something Chuck knew deep down couldn't be the fuel he would need to take care of those God would place within his sphere of influence. Chuck knew the two things he would need would be faith and family. Yesterday, Chuck Jr. lifted his forearm to show me his tattoo that read "Faith and Family." Now, tattoos might have been more on the back burner than the front burner when Jesus spoke of faith and family, but still Jesus said faith and family are the two most important things any of us can stand for.

You see, a guy once asked Jesus, "Jesus, if there's one thing that anybody could ever do right in this world, what would it be?" Now, this guy was trying to trick Jesus into saying something wrong, but Jesus called the man's bluff and when the Savior gave the answer, He doubled down and won the entire pot. "The greatest commandment," Jesus said, "is to love the Lord your God with all your heart, all your soul, all your mind, and all your strength. And the second is like it, you must love your neighbor as yourself." There it was: just like Chuck Jr.'s tattoo says, just like the one thing you told me Chuck stood for above all else, Jesus says we must have faith in Him as the Savior of us all, and we have to love the people God puts in front of us with every single part of who we are. Faith and family.

Yes, Chuck loved tow shows and seeing all the new equipment that was coming down the pike and visiting with all the other wrecking company owners. Yes, Chuck loved Ocean City, Hawaii, Disney World, and he even dipped his toes in the waters of Vegas a time or two. Chuck loved filet mignon from Outback, the Olive Garden and the Rio Grande, and was always more than willing to proudly display his filet mignon gut. But more than anything, Chuck loved the hard work he was engaged in and each of you. He took care of you no matter what. He was a good son. He was a great father and husband. If I may quote Chuck's mother, Lucille, "Chuck turned out to be a good boy."

Yes, Lucille, you're right. Your son has worked hard and cared for many. Chuck was always right there. And now I say to each of you, it's your turn to be right there, too. Caring for those God places in our paths is the responsibility of everyone. Sometimes God puts a lot of people in front of you like He did for Chuck, and other times God puts a handful of folks in front of you. Regardless of whether the number of people entrusted to your care is few or many, it is your responsibility to be right there for them, too. And when you're there, the two best things you can show up with is faith in the Savior and a protective, need-meeting love for your family.

Look to Chuck's example. Do greater things than you could ever imagine. Over time, release the bitter and become better. Be defined by this one you have lost.

May the peace and blessings of our God rest upon Chuck and each of you this day.

CHAPTER VI

WHY?

It is not an uncommon occurrence to receive a call from any funeral director requesting my services to officiate a funeral for a family who does not have a preacher of their own. All of us who make our living in ministry receive these requests. Still, when I received this call to officiate the funeral of Charlie Steringer, it was a call that broke my heart and then in the weeks following the funeral life just continued to go even more wrong.

When I received the call in August of 2016, I asked them to tell me about the deceased. The funeral director said to me, "Kevin, this one is very sad. He was a young man in his thirties who had gone on a fishing trip. Good guy ... no substance abuse issues ... no foul play. He just went to his tent after a day of fishing and never woke up the next morning. It's very sad. He is married with a very young son, and his wife is pregnant with their second child. She is due within the month."

I was sick.

These are the worst funerals to be asked to perform. The family at best is numb and at worst is angry. You pray that God will give you words of hope, and until God does, loving kindness and compassion must become the rule of the day.

125

As I often do, I told my mom about the service prior to meeting with the family. My mom said she knew both Charlie and his wife, Marissa, he was leaving behind. They were both students of hers when she was teaching world cultures at Morgantown High School. She told me she did not know Charlie as well, though he was well known as a great football player; but my mom said, "I loved Marissa. She was always one of my favorites." So with that information alone, I headed to the funeral home to meet with the family prior to the initial wave of people arriving at the visitation.

Marissa was very pregnant, and very sad, but she was not alone. Family and friends surrounded her. And right by her side was her little boy and her deceased husband's parents. My heart broke for them all.

*I asked them what I ask every family: "I don't want you walking out of here tomorrow saying, 'I wish Kevin would have said **this** about Charlie.' Tell me the **this** and I will put it all together for you."*

As best they could, they told me.

When such a young man dies, there is more silence shared than anything else.

*What follows is the **this** about Charlie Steringer I put together for Marissa, their son, and Charlie's parents.*

A great many were there.

The eulogy of Charlie Steringer

One of Marissa's favorite school teachers happens to be my mom, and while I never had the chance to meet Charlie there is a poem by Samuel Walter Foss that my mother taught me that seems to fit Charlie's character perfectly.

Why?

There are hermit
souls that live withdrawn
In the peace of their self-content;
There are souls, like stars, that dwell apart,
In a fellowless firmament;
There are pioneer souls that blaze their paths
Where highways never ran;
But let me live by the side of the road
And be a friend to man.

Let me live in a house
by the side of the road,
Where the race of men go by—
The men who are good and the men who are bad,
As good and as bad as I.
I would not sit in the scorner's seat,
Or hurl the cynic's ban;
Let me live in a house by the side of the road
And be a friend to man.

I see from my house
by the side of the road,
By the side of the highway of life,
The men who press with the ardor of hope,
The men who are faint with the strife.
But I turn not away from their smiles nor their tears—
Both parts of an infinite plan;
Let me live in my house by the side of the road
And be a friend to man.
I know there are brook-gladdened
meadows ahead
And mountains of wearisome height;
That the road passes on through the long afternoon

And stretches away to the night.
But still I rejoice when the travelers rejoice,
And weep with the strangers that moan,
Nor live in my house by the side of the road
Like a man who dwells alone.

Let me live in my
house by the side of the road
Where the race of men go by—
They are good, they are bad, they are weak, they are strong,
Wise, foolish—so am I.
Then why should I sit in the scorner's seat
Or hurl the cynic's ban?—
Let me live in my house by the side of the road
And be a friend to man.

(*The House by the Side of the Road,* Samuel Walter Foss)

I am told that Charlie was certainly a friend to man. Yesterday as Marissa, Carroll, Carolyn, Cathy, and I sat talking about Charlie, Carolyn said, "You know the television show, *Everybody Loves Raymond*? Well, everybody loves Charlie." I was not surprised by Charlie's mother's characterization of her son. From the time I learned of Charlie's passing, I have heard report after report of Charlie's greatness, and I am told by the folks from McCulla's that the online condolences have come in droves. A larger response is not uncommon when a young person passes, but in Charlie's case the outpouring of love and support is equal to the great love with which he blessed each of you.

Why does everyone love Charlie? Charlie lived as a friend to man, loving his family, his friends, his sports, the outdoors, his coworkers, and, despite the volatility they possess, the inmates he watched over. Though this quiet man only spoke out when he needed to, Charlie's loving character resonated loudly with each of you and many others in our community we may never even know.

As I sat and listened to Charlie's family yesterday, I took over four pages of notes concerning Charlie the husband, daddy, son, brother, friend and coworker. The thing I wrote down more than anything was, "Charlie was a very good daddy... Charlie was a very good husband... Charlie was a very good brother... Charlie was a very good son... Charlie was a very good uncle... Charlie was a very good grandson... Charlie was a very good friend." Most people in life understand how difficult it is to get one of these roles to the status of very good, but to achieve very good status with each of these relationship mantles, Charlie must have been deeply committed to the art of fashioning solid relationships. Most relationships are held together by proximity. If we are close geographically to a person we have a relationship, but when the individual moves out of our spheres of influence the relationship ends. From what I gather about Charlie, his commitment to relationships was a lifetime commitment. Charlie understood that neither good days nor bad days, prosperity nor difficulties should ever be allowed to define unity with individuals who have been divinely placed in our paths. Charlie knew that even disagreements were not a license to be disagreeable. Behind his Willie's Roadhouse exterior, Charlie's interior was committed to transparency, vulnerability, and courage so that he could reach the true self of every person he was blessed with the opportunity to stand before. Is it any wonder many of Charlie's kindergarten classmates are present here today? Friendships weren't ships passing in and out of Charlie's horizons. Charlie made friends and then kept friends through school, football, and every workplace he ever found himself. I'm not sure who said it yesterday, but I was told Charlie's many friends were lifetime friends.

Charlie's greatest friendship began on December 23, 2011. I asked Marissa yesterday to tell me the love story between her and Charlie, and when I did, she got a bit of a sheepish grin on her face. I wasn't surprised. I have found over the years that when the preacher asks a person to tell the truth, the whole truth and nothing but the truth, people have a tendency to get a bit nervous. Let's not forget I grew up in my dad's machine shop long before I ever stepped behind a pulpit. So, with a wink and a nod, I let Marissa off the hook, "What bar did you all meet in?" Exhaling, Marissa smiled and said, "Buck's."

While God's standard of holiness is never to be lowered, may we never forget Jesus' first miracle was turning water to wine at a wedding reception and Psalm 104:15 says, "[God] causes...wine which makes man's heart glad." (Psalm 104:14, 15 NASB) The fact that you two met at Buck's is ultimately irrelevant. It's what we do with the love and opportunities God blesses us with that matters.

So, regardless of the meeting place, Marissa and Charlie fell in love, were blessed with Grayson and one another, and in September another blessing will be before us. Anyone can have a spouse and some children, but to make a home is something far different. Ceremony and governmental paperwork generate a marriage, and biology creates a family. But a home...now that is something far different. Loving one's granny and pap and carrying on their legacy as you make their home your home is true family. Wrestling with your nephews and your son, but always being gentle, tender, and caring during the match is depth of relationship. Working an exhausting job all day but never being too tired to have a catch with your son when you get home is loving fatherhood. Having a wife who says, "Charlie was far too good to me," stands as a standard for us all. When I read in the obituary, "But Charlie's favorite activity was going to Black Bear games to watch his son run the bases," I thought there's not a son in the world who doesn't want his dad watching him run, and every father should hold their son's racing as his greatest activity.

Everything I have described to you are the opportunities each of us have for the greatest of human relationships, but sadly not everyone seizes the opportunity. Charlie, though, never allowed an opportunity for the most sacred of human relationships to ever pass him by.

I thought it was quite fitting yesterday for Charlie's dad to say, "Charlie was not only a hard worker, he was a great worker." I think you can discern from what I've said that Charlie worked on his personal relationships. But it seems to me that Charlie valued the platforms upon which he had been placed to foster these relationships. I was told that Charlie loved the outdoors, hunting, fishing, golfing, and football; that he cheered on the Mountaineers, the Pirates, and the Penguins; that Charlie worked as a prison guard with the Bureau of Prisons in Hazelton. Because Charlie had depth of relationship with people in each of these places, I am certain he understood the importance of the arena for friendships in which he had been placed. Follow my logic through the example Charlie's parents gave me yesterday.

They told me that Charlie loved football and that he developed friendships as he played for the Marilla Mustangs. The relationships Charlie made with the Marilla Mustangs didn't go away when he began playing for the South Stallions; instead, the relationships Charlie had were expanded. The same followed suit when he went on to Morgantown High School. As a Morgantown High School graduate myself, I understand how Mohigans are Mohigans regardless as to whether an individual has come from South, Suncrest, Westwood, or Mountaineer Middle. That's why those of us who graduated from MHS bleed red and blue, and for at least one week in the fall we … dislike strongly … a certain school in this community. When a person understands sphere of influence and the platforms for sphere of influence, he does everything he can to maintain those platforms. To Charlie, each of these schools were platforms to build strong friendships. Is it any wonder when Charlie got scholarship offers to play football at Glenville State and Fairmont State, Charlie politely declined. Charlie knew the platform that would expand his relationships and his positive influence was West Virginia University. At WVU, Charlie would major in psychology and move to an even deeper depth of the individual's heart and mind.

Charlie got his degree in psychology from WVU, and while I don't know all of his work history, Charlie became a correctional officer at Hazelton.

Keep walking with me and see Charlie's greatness.

I am told that Charlie was called "The Inmate Whisperer" at Hazelton.

I am told he could speak to prisoners whom no one else could get through to. Some would say it was his quiet demeanor. Others would say it was Charlie's understanding that we have been blessed with two ears and one mouth, so we should listen twice as much as we talk. But what we must all realize is Charlie's understanding that it is a gentle answer that turns away wrath. It's the old saying, "I don't care how much you know if I don't know how much you care." You can't trick someone into lasting trust. It is only those who are genuine, transparent, vulnerable, and courageous with whom we will be the same. Charlie was that while working at Hazelton and when he was with each of you. When you and they were lions, Charlie stood as the lamb. When you and they stood ready to fight with swords, Charlie had a beautiful way of beating those swords into plowshares. Charlie never complained. Charlie was just a friend, and friendship is the only weapon that cannot be overcome.

Dear friends, I hope each of you see the blessing you have had before you for a time far too short. I have said this many times before, but I say it with great seriousness here today: we are defined by those we have lost. I know very few people in life who are committed to depth of relationship. Jesus says it is easy to love those who love you, but difficulty comes when we offer love to those who offer hate, when we offer blessing to those who offer curses, when we offer prayers for those who spitefully use us. Charlie's commitment to depth of relationship, his willingness to be a true friend, must from this day forth define us all.

My prayers are with Marissa, Grayson, and the new baby. My prayers are with Carroll and Carolyn. My prayers are with Cathy and all the rest of Charlie's family members. My prayers are with each of you his friends and coworkers. My prayers are with those inmates with whom Charlie was a friend. But above all, my prayers are with each of us, that we do as Christ has commanded us to be: a friend to man just as Charlie has lived. Let us be defined by this one whom we have lost.

May the peace and blessing of our God rest upon Charlie and each of you this day.

When Charlie's funeral ended, we left the funeral home and drove high atop one of West Virginia's many hills. We certainly are no comparison to the youth of the Rocky Mountains, but there is a respect for the age of West Virginia's hills that must be had as any individual drives up Summer School Road all the way to the knoll called Nicholson Chapel. It was in the cemetery adjacent to Nicholson Chapel where we buried Charlie.

I don't remember if it was a beautiful day, but amidst sorrow's fog, from that knoll we could see all of Monongalia County and all the way into Pennsylvania.

I spoke the words I always speak during committal services.

My funeral director friends spoke their recitation and symbolically released Charlie's spirit back to God on the wings of a dove.

Then we all returned to our cars. Some of us easily stepped back onto the carousel of life. One was forced to ... she had to deliver her child in a few weeks.

Now, there is a lady in my congregation named Leah who is dear friends with Marissa. When Marissa had her baby, Leah told me.

While I hadn't forgotten about Marissa, her grief, and her pregnancy, sadly after finishing one tragedy, there is always the next tragedy that awaits. Those of us in the ministry do our best to keep track of those to whom we have ministered, but oftentimes only breath-prayers can be offered for them because our full attention is needed elsewhere. With this news of a safe and healthy birth, baby, and mom, it was a comfort knowing that the birth of Arya Marie Steringer could be a bit of salve to the wound of Charlie Steringer's death.

A few Sundays later as our 9:00 a.m. worship service ended, with a smile on my face I walked up to Leah and said, "How are Marissa and that new baby girl doing?"

The look on Leah's face made my heart sink.

"What's wrong, Leah?"

Leah was already crying.

"Leah?"

"Kevin," Leah said, "they're going to be calling you. Arya died in her crib. It was SIDS."

Less than two months after I buried Marissa's husband, I would now be laying her daughter Arya to rest.

I'm not really even sure why I am writing this, but I think it is important for you to know how to say Arya's name. It is pronounced, "Au-ree-uh."

You will see I spell it phonetically in the eulogy.

You'll also see I tell the china doll story my granny told me.

When a china doll has been broken beyond repair, it is important to help people cry ... and to pronounce the name of the china doll correctly.

The eulogy of Arya Steringer

More than twenty-five years ago, I was asked to serve my first four churches as a pastor. I had been preaching since I was sixteen, but an occasional Sunday here and there in the pulpit is distinctly different from serving four small country churches. And I was only twenty-years-old.

My grandmother was the daughter of a circuit-riding pastor. Her dad, my great-grandfather, at one time had eleven churches to which he traveled on horseback. With no clue myself, I figured my grandmother could give me sound advice. I said to her, "Granny, I can preach a pretty good sermon, and I think I know the Bible pretty well, but what do I say to a family who has lost a loved one, especially when that loved one is only a child?" My grandmother looked at me with a gentleness and told me a story I will never forget.

"There once was a little girl," my grandmother said, "who was late returning home from school. It wasn't a long time past when she was to return home, so the little girl's mother had no reason for alarm, but soon the minutes turned into an hour, and the hour turned into hours. Something wasn't right. The little girl had sauntered home from time to time, but had never been this late before. Immediately the mother began calling house after house asking if any of the other moms had seen her little girl. Every time the same answer: no. So, the mother left her home and searched for her daughter through the entire neighborhood. Still, no luck. The little girl could not be found. With pain in her heart and tears in her eyes, the mother returned home hoping to find her daughter there. The mother pushed the kitchen screen door open hoping to see her daughter sitting at the kitchen table, but once again her hopes went unrealized. The mom sat down at the kitchen table broken and with her head in her hands. Then the screen door opened and slammed. It was the little girl. The mother immediately scolded her, saying, 'Where have you been?! Didn't you know how worried I have been?!' Yet, the sight of seeing her daughter softened the anger. The mother listened as her daughter began telling her the reason for her lateness. 'Mommy, when I got off the school bus today, one of my best friends pulled the most beautiful china doll from her backpack. It was the most beautiful doll I had ever seen. We sat down and played with her for the longest time. We talked with her, cradled her, and then my friend stood up to dance with her. Then the most awful thing happened. As my friend was spinning with the doll, she lost her grip and the china doll fell to the ground and broke into a million pieces.' The mother saw the sadness in the little girl's eyes and knew of her caring heart, so she interrupted her daughter, saying, 'Oh, I understand, you stayed to help your friend put the pieces of the doll back together again?' The daughter just looked at her mother sadly, shaking her head. 'No, Mommy, the doll couldn't be put back together again. I just stayed and helped my friend cry.'"

Then my grandmother looked at me and said, "Kevin, sometimes there are no words you can ever speak that will bring comfort to the hurting. When you find yourself in those times, just help people cry." My grandmother was, and remains, right up to this day. There are no words that can be spoken to ease your pain. So I guess it is time to be arms to lean into and shoulders to cry upon.

I read the obituary for (Au-ree-uh) this morning. And I can only imagine how great a big brother Grayson has been. And I know the spoiling of (Au-ree-uh) already began by each of you. Jesus called children little lambs, and I can only imagine how you have each cared, loved, and showered your blessings upon this picture of the purity of our Christ. My shoulder and arms are here for you.

Dear friends, I have prayed for healings for those that I love many times before. Sometimes they have been granted life. Other times I have had to lay those I love the most to rest. I never understand it. I'm never content with it. Still, in a very strange way that I cannot explain, in the midst of unanswered prayer and the worst tragedies, my faith seems to strengthen rather than falter, even when I am angriest before God.

One of my dearest friends in the world died Saturday afternoon. He was not yet sixty. I will be burying him tomorrow. While remembering Dennis, a friend of mine quoted Psalm 90:4 which declares, "For a thousand years in Your sight are like yesterday when it passes by, or as a watch in the night." (Psalm 90:4 NASB) My friend looked at me and said, "Dennis has been gone from us for twelve hours. If this Scripture is true, then Dennis has already been in Heaven for 500 years." I have thought about that and thought about that.

Another young friend of mine, just hours before his death, looked at me and said, "Kevin, as soon as my mother got to Heaven I will be there, and as soon as I get there you will be there too."

A thousand years are like a day.

A soon as I get there, you will be there too.

None of us are content here today. All of us are broken. Some are falling into the arms of the sturdy and also crying on their shoulders. Yet in the midst of sorrow, somehow we must see eternity. (Au-ree-uh) is already 6,000 years old, and in the blink of an eye we can be there too. I'm glad God's math is not like the math of this world. Even in the midst of our greatest tragedies, God's math holds an eternal hope. While

(Au-ree-uh) will never return to us, we can certainly go to her. She has lived to a very young age here, but she is already very old there. In the few short years that we have left, why don't we help one another cry for a season and then live out our days, no matter how long or short they are, in such a way that we will return to this little lamb.

There is brokenness here.

There is beauty there.

We will cry with one and celebrate with the other.

May the peace and blessing of our God that rests upon (Au-ree-uh) rest upon each of you this day.

CHAPTER VII

NEEDLE FALL DOWN

One Christmas morning, a man walked up to me after our mid-night prayer service ended and said to me, "Kevin, there was a man who was just here looking for you. He left this letter for you. I tried to get him to stay and talk with you, but he wouldn't. Here's the letter."

The letter was sealed and in an envelope. As the last few people were leaving the sanctuary to head home for a few hours of sleep before the Christmas Day activities began, I slid my fin-ger under the envelope's seal, pulled out the letter, and began reading it.

It was unsigned, but I knew who had written it and the man who had left it for—"One of the pastors." The author and the leaver-of-the-letter were one-and-the-same man. It was my friend, Kenny. He and his wife were recently divorced, and he was alone this Christmas.

As I began reading the letter underneath a wall sconce, now all alone in the dark Christmas morning sanctuary, Kenny walked in. I never finished the letter, and I cannot remember any of the parts that I read. We talked until 2:30 in the morning. As we finished, I asked Kenny if he was okay to head home. He told me he was, and so after praying with him, I walked him to the door.

I went home to my family.

Kenny would be joined by his sons that Christmas evening.

Between 2:30 on that Christmas morning and early March of the next year, I saw Kenny a number of times.

He was very shaky, and I was more than worried about him. I met with him.

He saw doctors and had many conversations with many people.

Kenny meant a great deal to me. Nearly ten years prior, Kenny was a self-avowed atheist. Yet, as his wife and sons began attending church, Kenny began a deep pursuit of the God Whose existence he denied. We had many conversations. Some were communal. Some were contentious. But on one summer evening when many from our church congregation had traveled to a neighboring county and a shallow, slow-flowing river for baptisms, after baptizing many folks, including all three of my sons, I looked up on the riverbank and there was Kenny.

He was the last to step in the Cheat River that summer evening. He walked in as a man everyone believed to be an atheist. He emerged from the waters as our brother-in-Christ.

Depression is haunting, and depression is partial neither to Christian nor atheist. So with ten-plus years from Kenny's baptism, and two-plus months from my Christmas morning conversation with Kenny, I arrived at the church for a March Morning Prayer service. I was the first to arrive, and there was a note taped to the door that simply had one name written upon it: "Kevin." Next to the taped letter was a compact disc of a band named Union Sound Treaty.

The letter was from Kenny.

Union Sound Treaty was Kenny's favorite band.

I opened the letter and read it all. These are the words exactly as they were typed to me:

"Kevin,

Thank you very much for everything you have tried to do for Melanie, myself, and the boys over the years. And for what you will do in the years to come.

Here is the CD from my favorite band. You may already have one, but I wanted to drop it to you just in case you did not get to listen to. Thank you.

Love and God's blessings upon you and yours.

Kenny"

Later that morning I received the call. Kenny had left letters all over town to those who loved him.

After he delivered the letters in the middle of the night, Kenny committed suicide.

One of the songs on Union Sound Treaty's album Kenny left for me is titled, "Needle Fall Down." The words of the song bleed with irony.

Time of the evening I pull out my gun
Prepared for what's after I pour something strong
I yearn for the rope and a lady's sweet voice
To sing me my last words I won't sing along

Needle fall down sing me a song it's been a long life
and it all went wrong
Needle fall down sing me a song it's been a long life
and it all went wrong

Record's playing spinning around
My butterflies flying and they won't fall down
Needle rises up and the sound it's all gone
Bending and fading past the gun on my throne

141

The song's lyrics are not a license, but they are the over-whelming reality of the hurting world in which we live and the people we are being called to pay attention to. I have been asked many times as to whether or not suicide damns someone to Hell. While an understandable question, it is a shortsighted one. The reconciliation Christ affords does not come and go in the family of God's children each time each sins. Certainly murder is sin, but lying is too. No one condemns to Hell a Christian who dies in the midst of a lie.

That being said, life is to be lived not taken. God should be in charge of life and death.

I miss my brother Kenny.

I know his family misses him too.

The eulogy of Kenny Wilson

L ike each of you, my heart is broken today.
As I read these words my mind thought back to the Kenny I have known and loved so much:

Kenny was a graduate of Morgantown High School, where he played baseball and learned a love of the arts. After high school, he enlisted in the United States Air Force serving state-side until 1997. After leaving the Air Force, Kenny returned to Morgantown to successfully complete a bachelor's degree at West Virginia University School of Business with a Bachelor's Degree in Information Technology. He was employed as an IT analyst with CACI of Chantilly, Va. He was a member, along with his family, of the Kingdom Evangelical Methodist Church in Westover, West Virginia. He was an avid outdoorsman and enjoyed spending time with his boys camping and fishing on his favorite piece of property in Reckarts' Mill near Cranesville, in Preston County, West Virginia. Most evenings you could find

Kenny enjoying a good campfire and gazing at the heavens deep in thought. He loved astronomy and the wonders of the universe. Kenny enjoyed all sporting events and was an avid Atlanta Braves fan. In his spare time he enjoyed sketching and painting. You could also find Kenny writing a poem from time to time. He enjoyed coaching, teaching, and training his sons in the various sports in which they participated. Kenny's love for the ocean was only surpassed by the enjoyment he received from the occasional family beach trips. Most of all, Kenny was a family man with a huge heart and a friend to all. His ultimate pride and joy was in that of his four children. All boys, ranging in age from five to fifteen.

Yesterday I told Kenny's dad that the words of memorial concerning his son were perfect. Too often obituaries do little to characterize the beauty and richness of an individual's life, but this dad's memorial of his son was perfect.

I know everyone in this room possesses his and her own frame of reference concerning Kenny, and in the years to come each of you can and will share with one another every victory that lifted the heart and every defeat that strengthened the heart. Yet, for now, these are my memories of Kenny. They are not exhaustive, but they are my own.

I met Kenny probably more than fifteen years ago, but Kenny came into my life face-to-face when his oldest son was having surgery at Ruby Memorial Hospital, if my memory recalls, I believe twelve years ago. We were in a waiting room on the second floor of Ruby Memorial Hospital. We are people of faith, and while faith was definitely present, it is far easier to practice faith outside of the vacuum of life's circumstances. We prayed in the waiting room. The surgery was a success. He stands as the picture of health before you today. When we are weak, God is certainly strong.

After that day, I saw Kenny casually from time-to-time, but my real relationship began with Kenny a few years after his son's surgery. Kenny came to me and our then Pastoral Care Minister. Kenny was trying to figure out just what he believed. Like so many, Kenny wondered where he fell, and because of his wisdom and search for truth, Kenny wanted to gather as many facts as possible before he placed his faith in Jesus as Messiah. Our Pastoral Care Minister and I both met with Kenny over and over again. In the midst of all those meetings, Kingdom held what was at the time her annual baptismal service deep in the heart of Preston County at a small family campsite along the banks of the Cheat River. It was a very special day for me personally because it was the day I would be baptizing all three of my sons. We drove and drove from Morgantown all the way to Rowlesburg, then we made a right and drove and drove some more. It seemed like we would never get there. Then we saw a small makeshift cardboard sign with a single helium balloon flying a few feet above it. The sign read, "Baptism," so we slowed down and made a hard left onto a road that literally pointed us 180 degrees in the direction we had just driven. I hope you can understand from my description the baptismal site was very far from Morgantown and not easily found.

Without getting into all the details of the baptism itself, suffice to say it was one of the proudest days of my life. This was the day that I baptized my three sons, the day when my sons became my brothers. We were finishing up. Everyone who had wanted to be baptized had been baptized. We were heading to the shoreline from the middle of the Cheat River when I looked up, and walking down the riverbank there he was. It was the man who months before didn't know, by his own admission, whether he should be characterized as an atheist, an agnostic, or a person who believed in God, but hadn't surrendered to Christ. Most certainly, though, he was a man who, by his own admission, had not repented and surrendered his heart to Jesus as Messiah and Lord. And there he was, standing by himself on the riverbank. He had come alone. Clearly, it was his own decision. He had not come to that river to appease anyone. There he was. He could have turned back anywhere along that long journey to parts unknown somewhere to the right of Rowlesburg. There he was. He could have driven right past that little makeshift cardboard sign with the helium balloon. There he was. Standing on a riverbank wondering, without saying, if we had time for one more baptism.

We did.

Our Pastoral Care Minister had worked so closely with Tommy, so if I remember correctly I stepped to the side, and as another baptismal assistant and I stood within an arm's length, Kenny was asked, "Do you repent from your sins and surrender your life to Jesus Christ as Lord and Savior?" There he was. Kenny said yes. In that moment Kenny Wilson surrendered his life to Jesus Christ.

Folks, I'm going to say something difficult here, so prepare yourselves.

Jesus teaches us three very important truths about this world that we are living in prior to His final return. He teaches us that while He has come to give us life and life more abundant, the enemy comes but to kill, steal, and destroy. Second, Jesus says when a house is swept clean the enemy will leave for a season until a more opportune time comes to return with reinforcements. And, finally, we live in a world where both wheat and tares are permitted to grow up together until the time of the harvest. If we pull up the tares before the time of the harvest, some of the wheat may be damaged. With those three truths before us, that is the only explanation I can give concerning the events of last week. But I believe Kenny's conversion was genuine, and as I will read in a moment, there is nothing that can separate us from the love of Christ.

I will always remember that day in the Cheat River outside of Rowlesburg.

I will always remember Kenny's infectious smile.

I will always remember that night in Bible study as Kenny was trying to answer the question I had asked concerning the Scriptures, the tears that were rolling down his cheeks, and his words that he spoke, "You all will just have to get to know that I am a crier." I will always remember Kenny's tears of passion for his Christ.

I will always remember the look on Kenny's face this past summer during MountainFest week when Kenny walked into Schmidtt's Saloon to hear Union Sound Treaty play a show, and he saw his pastor sitting at a table in the bar getting ready to listen to Union Sound Treaty too.

I will always remember our talk until 2:30 this past Christmas morning immediately following Kingdom's Midnight Prayer Service.

I will always remember Kenny's final words to me.

I will treasure forever Kenny's final gift to me of a Union Sound Treaty CD case and the CD inside.

Overwhelming grief stands as the greatest shroud of eternal truth. I can promise you all of the light from Kenny's eyes and all of the abundance from Kenny's heart stood with him as he stood before the Lord.

And now you stand. How has and how will Kenny's life and passing forge the rest of your days?

One of my favorite writers is a woman named Ann Voskamp. She is the daughter of a Midwestern farmer, and now as an adult, is not only the farmer's daughter but a farmer herself. In her most recent book, *The Broken Way*, Voskamp tells of a childhood lesson her farmer father once taught her in the midst of a tragedy. She writes:

"[Daddy] pulls me into himself, enfolds me. And then, into the quiet, he says it so soft I almost miss it, what I have held on to more than a thousand times since.

'You know—everything all across this farm says the same thing, you know that, right?' He waits till I let him look me in the eye, let him look into me and all this fracturing. 'The seed breaks to give us the wheat. The soil breaks to give us the crop, the sky breaks to give us the rain, the wheat breaks to give us the bread. And the bread breaks to give us the feast. There was once even an alabaster jar that broke to give Him all the glory.'

He looks right through the cracks of me. He smells of the barn, the dirt, and the sky, and he's carrying something of the maple trees at the edge of the woods—carrying old light. He says it slowly, like he means it: 'Never be afraid of being a broken thing.'"

Dear friends, in our midst there is much brokenness and many broken things. Yet with the breaking comes harvest. With the breaking comes the aroma of the King … and in the midst of the fracture, that aroma is comfort and hope.

Finding the safety of our God within the deepest sadness is the most difficult of callings each of us face. Nearly a month ago while watching the morning news, I heard a father say of God concerning his missing and feared to-be-dead son, "If God cares, He will bring my son back to me." That father is right in his emotions, but wrong in His estimation of God's perfect character.

King David sings the funeral dirge best while emerging from the mourning at the loss of his infant son: "But now he has died; why should I fast? Can I bring him back again? I will go to him, but he will not return to me." (2 Samuel 12:23 NASB)

The most difficult thing to do is to eat a celebratory meal while being clawed at by the talons of heartbreak. Fasting seems far more fitting. Yet, in the midst of the bruising and the smoldering, we must look to the character of God, which declares, "A bruised reed He will not break and a dimly burning wick He will not extinguish." (Isaiah 42:3 NASB) And that same God says, "Who will separate us from the love of Christ? Will tribulation, or distress, or persecution, or famine, or nakedness, or peril, or sword? Just as it is written,

'FOR YOUR SAKE WE ARE BEING PUT TO DEATH ALL DAY LONG; WE WERE CONSIDERED AS SHEEP TO BE SLAUGHTERED.' But in all these things we overwhelmingly conquer through Him who loved us. For I am convinced that neither death, nor life, nor angels, nor principalities, nor things present, nor things to come, nor powers, nor height, nor depth, nor any other created thing, will be able to separate us from the love of God, which is in Christ Jesus our Lord."

(ROMANS 8:35–39 NASB)

This is the God Who holds all of us now, be you parent, son, sibling, wife, family, friend, or brother-in-Christ who witnessed his baptism. This is the God Who says He will turn thorns into mighty cypress trees and thistles into the most beautiful of myrtles. This is the God who, in the silence, whispers to you with the same voice with which He spoke to Elijah, saying, "What are you doing here?" This is the God Who said, "I will not leave you comfortless." This is the God Who knows the death of a Son and also His resurrection to Life, and the resurrection to Life for all those who have, by belief in his heart and profession of his mouth, surrendered to Him as Messiah.

It is Messiah who said to them then and says to us still, "The hour has come for the Son of Man to be glorified. Truly, truly, I say to you, unless a grain of wheat falls into the earth and dies, it remains alone; but if it dies, it bears much fruit. He who loves his life loses it, and he who hates his life in this world will keep it to life eternal." (John 12:23-25 NASB) Those who have stored up treasures in Heaven and smile from the abundance of their hearts are those who know true Life. God has never consulted me on any person's eternal standing, but I know that those who stand in the presence of God are smiling greatly, for the joy of the Lord is their strength.

I prayed prior to this eulogy reciting the words of Psalm 19:14 which say, "Let the words of my mouth and the meditation of my heart be acceptable in Your sight, O Lord, my rock and my Redeemer." (Psalm 19:14 NASB) I pray that these words of memorial concerning Kenny and honor to God have been just that.

May the peace and blessing of our God rest upon Kenny and also upon each of you this day.

CHAPTER VIII

ORDINARY FOLK ... EXTRAORDINARY LIVES

Not every funeral service officiated and eulogy offered is the product of a tragedy. Sometimes death just comes. It is no less painful, no less grief-worthy. Still, death arriving for a fine life lived, in many respects, is a beautiful thing. When existence is lived for life and not death, a settledness with passing in those who remain is very often present. There are still sadnesses for things left unsaid and undone, but the hurts between the deceased and those who mourn are more likely to be equated with the grass-stained good pants of playing children who return home to mother than they are to be the drooped heads and hunched shoulders of condemnation of teenagers with defiance on their breath caught sneaking in late after curfew. Appalachians have a term to characterize the simple best among us. The term is: Good People.

The following are eulogies of three Good People who spent their occasionally grass-stained days living for life.

Sharon Chapman was my senior English teacher in high school. The first eulogy offered in this section is for her mother,

Mary Toothman. It is a bit intimidating writing the eulogy for the mother of your senior English teacher. It is even more intimidating preaching it. In addition to the pressure of carrying out senior-English-lessons-long-ago learned, Mary Toothman was also a tough Appalachian wife of a cabinet-making husband. Her standards were high, and the wooden spoons in her hands were not only used to play the hammered dulcimer. Mary was but five-foot-nothing, yet she held to standards higher than her stature.

I did my very best with her eulogy.

When the service ended, my teacher said she was pleased. I trust Mary, looking in from the other side, was equally contented.

Next, there is Dave Felton.

I do not know whether this company has a presence where you live, but in the hills of West Virginia, the company called Life Is Good in many places has their message alive and well. One of the company's shirts is leisurely emblazoned with the advice that says, "All who wander are not lost."

Dave Felton wore a Life Is Good t-shirt to church every single week.

With his t-shirts, Dave would typically wear a pair of cargo shorts, sandals, and a small cross earring in his ear. He had John Lennon glasses and always a smile. He was a school teacher in one of West Virginia's most rural counties, Preston County.

Every summer, Dave always made available his family's campsite adjacent to the Cheat River so that our local church, and many others, could have baptismal services. My own sons were baptized there.

Dave lived his life as the best of fathers, husbands, brothers, teachers, and friends. Yet, above all, Dave Felton was a man of God. And, as a result of a life well-lived, Dave has heard those words we all long to hear, "Well done, good and faithful servant. Enter into your rest."

The final eulogy offered in this grouping of the extraordinary ordinary is the eulogy of my dear friend's mother, Mary Ellen Colombo.

Sadly, I only met Mary Ellen the last few years of her life. We had few conversations, but the ones we had are among those I most treasure. Her grandson and granddaughter were two of the teenagers to whom my wife and I have brought the Gospel. In the ministry of the Gospel, it is a natural thing to find parents and grandparents drawing closer and closer when a consistent message is being spoken to the children entrusted to their care. Mary Ellen was no exception.

From youth Bible studies for her grandchildren, soon Mary Ellen and her husband, Dr. Dino Colombo, found themselves weekly at our church packing lunch boxes full of meals to send home with hungry children from our local grade school. The kids at Skyview Elementary were mostly below the poverty line and nearly all on free and reduced breakfast and lunch, and the Colombo family was intent to see that those nearly three hundred kids to whom we provided eight weekend meals in a little blue lunch bag were not going to go hungry. Mary Ellen and Dino could have been doing many different things in their retirement, but instead they dedicated much of their lives to kids they would never meet.

As Mary Ellen began to grow weaker from cancer, I went to visit her in our university hospital. It was only she and I that morning. I, sitting in a chair. Mary Ellen lying peacefully in her hospital bed. The conversation was simple and honest. I find those conversations to be the best kind.

Mary Ellen died soon after that.

She lived in a city thirty miles south of my West Virginia town, so she had a pastor. He was the primary officiant of her service. The family asked me to offer the eulogy.

151

I give you that geographical and religious context for a reason. I am a bit of a hillbilly preacher, and hillbilly preachers are always far more concerned with their education than they are their schooling—though I have been schooled. That being said, when I got to the church where the service was being held, I introduced myself to the officiating pastor who was dressed in all his robed regalia. As I told him who I was, he looked at me and said, "Keep it brief. You people can go on forever."

I wasn't concerned with his admonition.

Every Appalachian lady deserves her day of honor. Suffice to say, the length of Mary Ellen's eulogy was consistent with her character and not the officiating pastor's dictum.

The eulogy of Mary Toothman

While we all live in Appalachia, I am not sure every individual has a love or an appreciation for the radiant glory the lady named Appalachia holds. Many speed through her mountains, look past her rivers, they never pause to appreciate her clothing of rocks and trees, nor do they breathe deeply her honeysuckle perfume. She is simply dismissed as a house-coated woman tainted by coal dust, who eats from an overgrown garden, and taps her toe to the homemade sounds of hillbilly rhythms.

Some would never consider asking the wallflower for a dance.

Yet some of us shuffle across the sawdust and with mustered courage say the words of the lyrical poet, Bob Dylan, "Wallflower, wallflower, won't you dance with me? I'm sad and lonely too. Wallflower, wallflower won't you dance with me? I've fallen in love with you."

Some of us want to marry the one named Appalachia.

I did not know Mary Toothman as well as anyone in this room, but I am sure I know enough about her to say she walked slowly through Appalachia's hills, she looked intently upon living waters, she paused to appreciate limestones and rhododendrons, and she knew what honeysuckle smelled like when through the air it wafted. And while I don't know for sure, I'm guessing Mary owned a housecoat and ate from an overgrown garden or two, and when she sat down behind her hammered dulcimer and told each of us to settle in for "a little bit of music," all were pleased with Mary to tap our toes to the hillbilly rhythms that are so much a part of our souls.

When I see Mary Toothman, I do not see a woman married to Appalachia; no, I see the lady Appalachia herself. Now Appalachia is a bit tough, and so was Mary at times, but her beauty is easily uncovered.

Yesterday as I asked Sharon what needed to be shared today, the first thing she spoke of concerning her mother was how deeply Mary loved and cared for her five siblings and their families, Mary's nieces and nephews. I read the names of those siblings this morning: Rensel, Elmer, Harry—who also went by June, Neva, and Frances—all very Appalachian names. I also noticed that Mary was the last remaining of her six siblings. I imagine as close as they all were in life growing up on the backdoor of the Great Depression and World War II, it was probably a bit heartbreaking for Mary to be the last of the remaining siblings. This eulogy is about Mary, not about my grandmothers who both outlived every one of their siblings, but from my grandmothers' experience I have learned to be the last remaining is not easy; and while the faithful know the road home, it is lonely when God has called the last ones to remain a little while longer. When there is an unwavering devotion to those who share blood, the devoted cry out as the apostle Paul did when he said, "But I am hard-pressed from both directions, having the desire to depart and be with Christ, for that is very much better; yet to remain on in the flesh is more necessary for your sake." (Philippians 1:23, 24 NASB)

Perhaps this is why Mary held so strongly to this world in her final days? Personal hopes and prejudices often occupy the same corners of the mind, but when a person is a Christian at heart, we must leave the mind's corners and return to the second half of Paul's statement that declares, "Convinced of this, I know that I will remain and continue with you all for your progress and joy in the faith, so that your proud confidence in me may abound in Christ Jesus through my coming to you again." (Philippians 1:25, 26 NASB) And as long as she needed to, Mary stayed.

That word "staying" is a powerful one. I know that Mary stayed and cared for her mother for more than nine years while her mother prepared to walk her heavenly road home. I know that Mary said to Sharon once, "If you marry a man half as good as your daddy, then you will have done well." Sharon stayed on her mother's staying advice and has more than stayed with her husband who has proven to be more than half. Sixty-one years stayed Mary and Lester in love and in marriage. Sixty-one years stayed the Toothmans' home on Marchand Drive. Perhaps the home has stayed so long because Lester laid every foundation stone himself and, with his own hands, built the home from salvaged boards from a former High Street church?

We joked earlier about Mary staying to play "a little bit of music." Still we must mention that Mary absolutely loved to play her hammered dulcimer. Russ Fluharty built her first one, and as crude as it was, Mary stayed at it under the tutelage of Patty Looman, a true Appalachian lady in her own right. Concerning playing mountain music: as I read Mary's obituary, I loved the line that said, "Mary also belonged to the Westside Civic Club and the Westside Senior Center where she especially enjoyed the Friday night jam session playing her hammered dulcimer with her brother Elmer playing his fiddle." Only in West Virginia does one find a man named Elmer with his fiddle in tow.

Now while I do not want to belabor this point of staying, I do want to speak of how Mary stayed with her son, Richard. There is always something about a mother and her son. I have felt mother's love personally, I have watched it play out with three sons of my own, and I have seen Sharon's love for her three sons. I learned yesterday that Richard was an Eagle Scout and that Mary's love stayed with Richard through the whole project, even requiring her at one point to consume rattlesnake. And while the consumption of rattlesnake may not be the most remembered component of Mary's love for her son, I was also told of how Richard once ran away from home to his father's cabinet shop a half-mile away.

When Mary located her son, let's just say she stayed on him ....with a switch the entire half-mile home.

We joke, but according to Richard, the Toothman home with a plate of Mary's chocolate chip cookies was the exact spot he and all of his childhood friends desired to be.

Appalachia isn't always the holler of the hills. Sometimes Appalachia is a hand-constructed home at the end of a street on the west side of the Monongahela River. Sometimes Appalachia is a hilltopper high school, a home church on Spruce Street and the Wayside Helpers Class. There's just something about a Methodist church in Appalachia, and it doesn't really matter whether it is the little brown church in the vale or not. It is still the church that is dear to our childhood. Appalachia is the one iced tea glass that every grandson desires to drink from, Nan's cornbread and that one special pan in which she bakes it, and her willingness to jump in the middle of her grandsons' Christmas morning scrum. Even Appalachian "Nans" know it ain't right to fight on Christmas Day. And while Appalachians may own a Starcraft camper and enjoy camping from Montreal to Alabama, there is no place like the West Virginia hills, how majestic and how grand.

Now the Appalachian lady has gone home.

There is no greater beauty as the beauty where you belong.

Dear friends, it matters not if we designate Mary as the Appalachian lady to be gazed upon or the wallflower we would all be wise to cross the dance floor and ask to dance the final dance of the evening. What does matter is that Mary's life should cause the rest of our lives to tap the toe to the sound of hillbilly dulcimer strings. This is the little job for us to do now. Mary has found her way home to the beauty where she belongs. Now the sounds of the dulcimer and the fiddle call us to do the same.

May the peace and blessing of our God that rests upon Mary also rest upon each of you this day.

The eulogy of Dave Felton

We always struggle to find the words during times like these. The reason for the verbal uncertainty is most likely to be found in our desire to speak rather than listen. My wise grandmother once told me that God gave us two ears and one mouth, so we should listen twice as much as we talk. I asked one question of Dave's family yesterday and then set my ears to listening. What they shared with me was the validity of one man's love for his Lord and for all those his Lord had placed in front of him.

As the listening began, the very first words to flow concerning Dave was his commitment to be an evangelist. Dear friends, I do many funerals annually, and I cannot tell you how rarely I hear evangelism as the primary, let alone the secondary, characterization of an individual's life. More often than not I hear very temporal qualities of individuals. For the advancement of the Gospel of Jesus of Nazareth to be the first thing unanimously offered from the mouths of those who lived by Dave's side day by day, I am overjoyed. This is the most substantive quality that could ever be present in any individual's life.

I'm told that the reason Dave's passion to witness Christ ran so deeply is because at twenty-one years old, Dave was miraculously healed of cancer. This man had a deep appreciation for his whirlwind birthday. This twin who was born in a speeding car in Maryland just after his seconds-older-sister had been born in West Virginia was granted a second chance to live a life for God as he entered the first throes of adulthood. It was reported to me that one day Dave possessed a cancerous tumor and no hope of life, and the next day the tumor had disappeared. So many of us would take the money and run, so to speak, but Dave was among the minority who choose to remain at the feet of the Healer after they have received their hoped-for-miracle. From that day on, Dave lived committed to sharing the Gospel with all those who would listen.

He never told me that story. I'm hoping that's because Dave assumed his pastor was squared away in the salvation department. But for the kids Dave taught for twenty-nine years, it was a simple cross earring that opened the conversation for how the exclusive Messiah for every nation, tribe, and tongue had saved and changed Dave's life, and how that same Lord was ready and waiting to save and change them.

Listening further, for Dave evangelism flowed to fatherhood. Follow this spiritual equation: Jesus commands us to call no man father, for we have but one Father Who is in Heaven. Jesus prays to His Daddy, his Abba, in the Garden of Gethsemane. Like Joseph to Jesus, we are to be Godly stewards over the children with which the Lord has entrusted and blessed us. As Christians, we possess the Spirit of God in our hearts. So if all this is true, and if we are surrendered to this truth, then as earthly fathers, our children should see Abba, Daddy, in us. Our lives as paternal patriarchs should point children to the Divine Daddy. Is it any wonder after evangelist and educator, the family characterized Dave as the best dad?

Dave may have been the best dad, but as to whether or not he was the best golfer is up for debate. Apparently home was a bit of a fourth choice for Dave, though he stood excellent in his role as family man. After school and the Gospel, it was the golf course at Paradise Lake that Dave found his sanctuary. I asked Dave's golfing buddies last night if Dave was a good golfer. His fellow legionnaires of the links told me they spent enough time watching Dave's moves on the golf course to confirm his excellence as reported on his scorecard. Perhaps Dave's golf prowess was a direct result of his commitment to change his swing annually and to video-selfie said swing change for the purpose of study.

It was so easy to love Dave.

He was, and remains, quite lovable. He epitomized the Gospel as he cared for every widow and orphan, as he took the orphans under his wings at school, and the widow cutting their yards until they had been reunited with their first loves. The glasses, the hat, the Life Is Good Shirts, the smile, the willingness to hand out bulletins in the parking lot rather than at the church door, the singing more loudly than anyone else, and the aforementioned cross earring, all of these things stand as the reasons Dave is so easy to love. Dave paddled through our lives with the same proficiency he kayaked the Cheat River Narrows, with an equal deftness to care for us backwards as well as forwards. When you love well enough for even the dog to feel he has reached the status of son, then you must be doing something right. Just ask Owen if he loves Dave.

When someone cares when he doesn't have to, it is surprising and sometimes even unsettling. Why would a man show compassion to a recently widowed lady he barely even knew? Why would a man offer a family campsite at the edge of the Cheat River so person upon person, including this pastor's three young sons, could be baptized making their public profession for Christ? When Jesus commands the righteous to come and receive their inheritance prepared for them from the beginning of the world, they will be equally shocked to receive this gift of God as we were to receive their no-strings-attached affection. They will say, *Lord, why are we deserving of such an inheritance?* Jesus tells those who are excellent at loving those around them that as they cared for widows, orphans, students, church people, golfers, family, and dogs named Owen, those individuals were actually caring for Jesus Himself.

Honestly, dear friends, what I heard about Dave yesterday somehow I already knew. Dave Felton made the very most of his moments, and his life now challenges us to do the same.

May the peace and blessing of our God that most certainly rests upon Dave rest upon each of us this day.

The eulogy of Mary Ellen Colombo

Just over two weeks ago on a Monday morning, Dr. and Mrs. Colombo along with their son gathered in my sanctuary for Kingdom's daily Morning Prayer service. Surrounded by brothers and sisters in Christ Mary Ellen had never met before, I anointed Mary Ellen with oil as the Scriptures prescribe in the book of James, chapter 5, verses 14 and 15.

With a cross of oil on her forehead, we laid our hands on Mary Ellen and prayed for the peace and strength of our Messiah to be upon her, and that the God in Whom we live, move, and have our being would grant Mary Ellen every single day He had prepared for her to share the Gospel. The prayer time continued and completed, and then the bleary-eyed, rag-tag band of the Lord's disciples gathered around the Colombos, offering them the peace of Christ.

Even though we all walked from our 6:30 a.m. daily prayer service back onto the carousel of life, in light of the anointing just completed, I could not stop thinking about the passage of Scripture in the twelfth chapter of John's Gospel that speaks of the anointing in Bethany. The Scripture reads:

Jesus, therefore, six days before the Passover, came to Bethany where Lazarus was, whom Jesus had raised from the dead. So they made Him a supper there, and Martha was serving; but Lazarus was one of those reclining at the table with Him. Mary then took a pound of very costly perfume of pure nard, and anointed the feet of Jesus and wiped His feet with her hair; and the house was filled with the fragrance of the perfume. But Judas Iscariot, one of His disciples, who was intending to betray Him, said, "Why was this perfume not sold for three hundred denarii and given to poor people?" Now he said this, not because he was concerned about the poor, but because he was a thief, and as he had the money box, he used to pilfer what was put into it. Therefore Jesus said, "Let her alone, so that she may keep it for the day of My burial. "For you always have the poor with you, but you do not always have Me."

(JOHN 12:1–8 NASB)

I have thought and thought about that verse in relation to Mary Ellen. You see, the verses from the book of James tell us our anointing leads to healing. Contrastingly, the verses from John's Gospel say anointing leads to burial. Still, both Scriptural anointings are evidence of full, sacrificial devotion to Jesus Messiah. With much meditation, I know now when Mary Ellen was anointed that Monday morning she was anointed as one bearing the very image of Christ. The fools of the world will speak such foolishness as "She lost her twenty-five-year battle with cancer." Still, it is the wise who sees and understands that as Mary anointed Christ, we anointed the Mary Ellen who has always bore her Savior's image. Over the days that followed the anointing that early morning, I realized that the Father's daughter has been saying to each of us what she has been living before us all her life, "You will always have the poor among you, but will not always have me."

Our Lord, Jesus of Nazareth, spent His entire life proclaiming good news to the poor, proclaiming freedom for the prisoners, bringing recovery of sight to the blind, setting the oppressed free, and proclaiming the year of the Lord's favor. Has Mary Ellen Colombo lived her life any differently than the Savior of the universe? Mary Ellen lived her life caring for the poor, proclaiming freedom to prisoners, bringing recovery of sight to the blind, setting the oppressed free, and proclaiming the year of the Lord's favor. She was anointed as our Christ, and said to each of us, "I have lived my life caring for the least of these our brothers and sisters. They will always be in this world, but I will not. So, see the legacy I have lived before you, and care for them as I, in the Spirit of Christ, have offered them care." Mary Ellen's anointing was appropriate, for this is the legacy she lived.

When I asked Dr. Colombo Tuesday night to tell me the one thing that had to be shared about Mary Ellen's life, he looked at me and said, "Fifty-seven years… so dependent on each other. She's gone and then you realize." Mary Ellen lived her life entertaining angels unaware, and now we realize we've been entertaining an angel. What began as a blind date between a not-yet-Dr. Colombo and a young Galloway, West Virginia girl turned into a life of care for many in this community.

I've known the Colombos for nearly ten years now, but not until the other night did I have any idea Mary Ellen was a first-grade school teacher. I wasn't surprised. Nor was I surprised Mary Ellen had a place in her heart for the rotten little boys heading towards the principal's office more so than the good little boys heading to the front of the classroom. It's the sick among us who need the doctors, not those who are well. Mary Ellen taught for only a handful of years while Dino was working his way through dental school, but in typical Mary Ellen fashion, she stayed in contact with all of her fellow teachers throughout her entire life. That was how it was with Mary Ellen: every relationship she had was engaged at the depth of relationship.

In our world, customarily it is proximity that keeps together the fragile bounds of come-and-go relationships, but not so with Mary Ellen. She was committed to maintaining the fraternity among those God brought within her sphere of influence, and she would never allow anyone whose heart she touched to ever be discarded because each person touched her heart.

It's interesting. Once Jesus was asked what the single greatest commandment is. Jesus turned to the man and said that the single greatest commandment is actually one commandment that is twofold. The Lord of the Universe said to the man, "'You shall love the Lord your God with all your heart, and with all your soul, and with all your mind.' This is the great and foremost commandment. The second is like it, 'You shall love your neighbor as yourself.'" (Matthew 22:37–39 NASB) We've come to know the second half of Jesus' admonition as the Golden Rule: Do unto others as you would have done unto you. This is good, but simply loving as we would want to be loved is relative to the individual offering his standard love. The standard of God can never be relative to each individual. Jesus understood this, and so while in the Upper Room, He offered additional clarification to His disciples and to each of us as to how our neighbors are to be loved. On that night before Jesus died for your sins and my sins, Jesus looked at His disciples and said, "A new commandment I give to you, that you love one another, even as I have loved you, that you also love one another." (John 13:34 NASB) The Son of Man who came to serve rather than be served tells us it is not enough to simply love with relativism. We must love divinely, and divine love is sacrificial love. Mary Ellen knew and exhibited what so few come to realize. Mary Ellen did nothing out of selfish ambition or vain conceit. Rather, in humility, Mary Ellen valued others above herself, never looking to her own interests but only to the interests of each of us. Be you old friend of ninety or one of her grandchildren's friends of sixteen, you were going to receive the sacrificial love of Jesus Christ from Mary Ellen Colombo. Even her entrepreneurial spirit that came alive in D & S Metalcraft was not motivated by greed. This hand-painted, nongalvanized steel bucket venture that ended up selling thousands of units to L. L. Bean and QVC was entered into in order to simply put her sons through graduate school.

As we sat Tuesday night in the Colombos' Bridgeport home of forty-five years, someone said, "She was awesome. She was the matriarchal glue for this family." Yes, the little lady who kept a wooden spoon in her pocketbook and who was deadeye with a penny loafer always had everyone's best interest in mind. I had heard of tall tales and supposed fables, but not until the other night was it confirmed that Mary Ellen was always the one who saw that every birthday, every holiday, every farewell and retirement party would be held in honor of those who needed to be honored. She opened her home in the Spirit of the First Century Church, always the first there and the last to take leave as she saw that everyone was included and everyone would have a good time. I'm even told that Mary Ellen at Christmas time would purchase extra gifts of the general but well-thought-out nature, so that when an unexpected guest would arrive at the party, they too would have a present to open.

Mary Ellen just loved people, and they in turn loved her back. And Mary Ellen was always looking for new opportunities to love her old and soon-to-be friends. At sixty years old, Mary Ellen decided to take up golf, and in typical Mary Ellen fashion, she became a champion at golf like so many other things before. But golf proficiency and excellence wasn't her goal. No, for Mary Ellen it was friendship. Yes, she ended up winning a club championship or two, but truth be told, Mary Ellen was just as happy parking her golf cart in sand traps and finishing as the bronze medalist while playing with the stereotypical three ladies who no one else had the patience to play with … my apologies to you three stereotypical ladies if you are in attendance today.

Some of the final folks who received Mary Ellen's love were 265 poverty-ridden school kids at Skyview Elementary on the west side of the Monongahela River. A few years ago, with the help of all the Colombos, we began sending the nearly 300 school students—who were on free and reduced breakfast and lunch at the Mon County School—home each weekend with a little blue lunchbox filled with nearly 3,000 calories of breakfast, lunch, dinner and snack foods. Dr. and Mrs. Colombo would drive to Westover week after week setting up the food for packing and distribution. They were the first ones to spell the hunger of these poor kids.

Is it any wonder Mary Ellen was anointed a little over two weeks ago? Sitting alone with Mary Ellen in her hospital room one week and a day ago, she looked at me and said, "I have lived a very good life. One of the greatest gifts anyone can have is a daughter, yet my husband and my sons who have cared for me with the greatest love and humility is beyond anything I could have ever asked." With those words I could see the peace in Mary Ellen's eyes. Then, just as peacefully, the door opened and in walked the man who has held Mary Ellen's hand for more than sixty years. Dr. Colombo told me yesterday to focus on Mary Ellen, but a tribute to her cannot be stated without a celebration of both parties of this matched set. Dr. Colombo has lived as a champion husband and father in partnership with the flesh of his flesh and stands as the best of examples of a sacrificially-loving husband and encouraging father to Dino, Steve, and all of us.

Jesus tells us that as this world passes away, all creation will be gathered before Him designated to stand on either the Messiah's left or right hand. To those on His right hand, the Scriptures say Jesus will bless, saying, "Come, you who are blessed of My Father, inherit the kingdom prepared for you from the foundation of the world. For I was hungry, and you gave Me something to eat; I was thirsty, and you gave Me something to drink; I was a stranger, and you invited Me in; naked, and you clothed

Me; I was sick, and you visited Me; I was in prison, and you came to Me." (Matthew 25:34–36 NASB) The Word then says those on Jesus' right will look to Him and say, "Lord, when did we see You hungry, and feed You, or thirsty, and give You something to drink? And when did we see You a stranger, and invite You in, or naked, and clothe You? When did we see You sick, or in prison, and come to You?" (Matthew 25:37–39 NASB) It is then Jesus says that He will simply say, "Truly I say to you, to the extent that you did it to one of these brothers of Mine, even the least of them, you did it to Me." (Matthew 25:40 NASB) Dear friends, the poor will always be with us, and in them will be the Spirit of Christ watching how we will care for Him. Mary Ellen lived her life caring for all of us and all of them, and so she stands appropriately anointed in the Presence of the Lord. Just like Jesus, if all the tales were to be told of Mary Ellen's love, all the books in all the libraries of the world could not contain them. It is now our responsibility to not only read the stories of Mary Ellen's days, but to be defined by the song of this sacrificial life that sings from the pages.

May the peace and blessings of our God that most certainly rests upon Mary Ellen also rest upon each of you this day.

CHAPTER IX

"I Forgive the Man Who Killed My Son."

Frank Hawkins is my dear friend and one of my earliest spiritual mentors.

Frank was a dad of three boys and one girl. The boys—Randy, Timmy, and Pat—all played baseball at our local little league park. Frank's daughter, Carol, did not.

Pat was my age. Timmy was two years older. Randy was older than us all. All three Hawkins boys could play ball, but Randy was the best. Sure, Pat was hitting home runs over the fence when he was seven years old, and Timmy with his golden locks, fastball arm, and big bat was an inspiration to many of us younger players, but it was Randy who stood as our ballpark's Superman. Randy was legendary, and from childhood to manhood, every son who would one day become dad idolized him.

Frank was proud of all his boys, but all of them, and all of us, knew it was Randy who earned and appropriately wore the coat-of-many colors.

Now no longer a kid, I was Frank's preacher, and I was Randy's preacher. They were two of my life's biggest heroes, and

I was honored and blessed to say I drew the straw that afforded me the opportunity to minister to them and their families.

With Frank, it was more of the teacher becoming the student, so that the student can learn how to teach.

With Randy, one night in my office with his wife by his side and tears in his eyes, he said, yes to the reconciliation Jesus' Gospel affords. It was my honor to lead Randy to Christ.

Not long after that evening, I was returning home from a denominational conference I had been required to attend. As I stood on the driveway unloading my bags, our small town's chief of police pulled up to my home. Chief Smith was also one of the now-men-once-little-leaguers who grew up at the park, and he too knew the Hawkins family very well.

From his cruiser, Jimmy said to me, "You just get home?"

His face didn't look settled and his words were shaky, so I immediately asked, "What's going on, Jimmy?"

"Randy got shot today," Jimmy said.

"What? Where is he? Is he okay?" I said, stunned.

With tears in his eyes, Chief Jimmy Smith said, "Kevin, he's dead."

I thought only kryptonite could kill Superman. Apparently, a careless turkey hunter hearing Superman's turkey call on the other side of some brush and then blindly shooting a shotgun into that brush at a nonexistent turkey can kill Superman too.

The hunter with Randy on the other side of that brush told me all Randy said was, "I'm shot." Then he fell over and died.

I sure am glad we prayed that prayer in my office that night.

You can imagine what the funeral was like. If you're discerning enough, you can see you've already read much about that day.

Well, many years later after I had more than a handful of conversations with Randy's dad, Frank, he ascended the steps at our church. I had asked Frank to preach a sermon. I heard him do so many times before.

Like every good preacher, Frank first opened his Bible and read us a Scripture.

I don't remember which Scripture it was.

Then he asked us to bow our heads and close our eyes, and Frank prayed.

The "In Jesus' name, Amen," came, and then Frank said these words...

"I forgive the man who killed my son."

While Frank preached with many more words that evening, he didn't need to say another thing. He'd made his point and all of us in attendance knew that we would need to always forgive now too.

How many times should we forgive, Lord? Seven?

I'm guessing to forgive the man who kills your son may take seventy times seven of forgiveness.

Frank forgave.

Forgiven, Frank lives in the place of forgiveness with his forgiven son.

This is the eulogy of my friend, my brother, and one of my greatest spiritual mentors, Frank Hawkins.

The eulogy of Frank Hawkins

"We got 'er made now, don't we?"

Those were the words Frank spoke to me last Tuesday when I arrived at his room at Sundale nursing home. Sadly, on this side of everlasting life, those were the next-to-last words my dear friend and brother will ever speak to me. Yet there in that first-floor room, I just looked at my old friend and said:

"Yes, Frank ... we certainly do have her made now."

I met Frank Hawkins when I was only a boy.

I was just a kid playing Little League at Westover Park. Like many others, Randy was my hero. Timmy was the hard-throwing pitcher two years my senior, and Pat was the only "B" Leaguer hitting over-the-fence home runs. At that stage of the game, Carol was a little girl sitting next to Frank and Judy with a baby doll in one hand and, like all of us kids when we weren't on the field playing, Carol's other hand held a snow cone with snow cone juice running down her arm and dripping from her elbow. I never was on a single team with the Hawkins boys, and Frank never taught me how to throw, catch, or hit, but the guidance Frank Hawkins had on my life began at that ballpark and, unbeknownst to Frank, grew passively through my twenties until, over nearly the last two decades, I have been blessed with the opportunity to be part of Frank Hawkins' circle of Christian influence.

Why does a man of God do what He does?

Each of us knows the characteristics that made Frank unique. He adored his family. He was never without a ball cap. He loved his ever-growing garden. He ate oranges when he wasn't supposed to. He was easily discovered at a baseball or softball field where his kids then grandkids were pitching, hitting, and fielding. He was watching the Pirates until his last day on this earth. He loved going to breakfast with his dear friends. We all are fully aware of what makes Frank distinct, but the true Christian who has influence does what he does for two very specific reasons: His actions are the natural extension of internal character, and his actions are the intentional example for those divinely placed before him. Maybe Frank did not understand this fully at the moment of his conversion, but Frank Hawkins grew to decipher the reason he was living as a man of God. Two Scriptures illustrate this truth:

"The good man brings out of his good treasure what is good; and the evil man brings out of his evil treasure what is evil."

(MATTHEW 12:35 NASB)

and

"Let your light shine before men in such a way that they may see your good works, and glorify your Father who is in heaven."

(Matthew 5:16 NASB)

When a man trusts in Jesus of Nazareth as Messiah, the Holy Spirit immediately and literally takes up residence in the man's heart, and then the Holy Spirit begins to visibly live through the man as evidenced in the man's Godly actions. This is why Jesus says, "A good man brings good things out of the good stored up in him." Only God is good, and the good flowing from the man surrendered to Christ is God Himself.

In addition, the Godly man's life is not solely being lived for the sake of goodness. The Godly man also is living intentionally visible for Christ, so that those who have been entrusted to his care may also trust in Christ as he has. And this is why Jesus says, "Let your light shine before men in such a way that they may see your good works, and glorify your Father who is in heaven." (Matthew 5:16 NASB) The blessing of everlasting life never finds its final destination in the one who has received it. Instead, when a man has experienced everlasting life, he knows he must shine it clearly to others that they may also choose to trust in Jesus for salvation.

Frank knew his internal nature and his responsibility to others. The Holy Spirit was very much alive in Frank as a result of his surrender to Jesus Christ as Lord, and Frank shared that with everyone with both unashamed words and with silent example. Frank is the same and distinct to all of us. God used Frank to give each one of us exactly what each one of us needed. Still, even when Frank ministered to each of us away from the rest of the world, there was always a consistent message that was reigning.

I believe each of us experienced the call to simplicity in Frank.

Can we really consider it an accident that the man of simplicity we honor today is simply named Frank? Franklin Delano Hawkins lived his life very frankly. It was Solomon who said in Ecclesiastes 7:29, "Behold, I have found only this, that God made men upright, but they have sought out many devices." (Ecclesiastes 7:29 NASB) Too many seek too many devices, but not Frank. Dear friends, I'm not sure I have ever met a man who was more understanding of the pursuit of the simple life than Frank Hawkins. We saw this pursuit as Frank would day after day wear the same Fairmont State baseball cap. We saw it as Frank was more than content to live in a simple house by Union Church Road for more than half a century. I saw simplicity one day recently at the hospital as Frank thoroughly enjoyed a number of spoonfuls of Cream-of-Wheat prepared in a hospital cafeteria. The key to simplicity is not leaving things but making the rule and reign of God our primary concern. Such is the reason Jesus said, "But seek first His kingdom and His righteousness, and all these things will be added to you." (Matthew 6:33 NASB) Now we know why Frank supported his children and grandchildren and why Frank enjoyed the Pirates, but he never allowed a ball or a ball game to become god over Christ. Frank's life was simple. His words were simple. He sought Christ first, and everything necessary for Frank was added unto him.

Frank Hawkins lived a life of simplicity.

Frank also offered a message of authority.

While standing at the foot of Frank's bedside last Wednesday, I leaned over and spoke very quietly to one of Frank's nieces. I said to her, "While Frank was never ordained and never earned a seminary degree, it is Frank who taught me more about pastoring than any pastor I have ever known." While God most certainly calls some individuals to further their education at institutions of higher learning, many individuals are called to learn the life of the ministry in the Judaean Wilderness so to speak. Many in this world look down on those who have been called in such a manner. The religious elite downplay the person's calling by saying they are actually protecting Christianity from false teachers, but their true intent is to keep those favored by God from exposing their lust for power and love for positions of authority. Those of us who have been called to the pastorate apart from seminary are honored that we have been called in such a manner, and we will protect to the death the sheep who have been entrusted to our care from the hirelings who attempt to steal, kill, and destroy.

Frank Hawkins is such a protector.

Frank never received the authority to baptize from men, but the commendation he received from God was more than sufficient to preach the Gospel of Jesus Christ. Without ordination, Frank preached, taught, baptized, offered Holy Communion, provided food for the hungry, drink for the thirsty, clothing for the naked, shelter for the homeless, and visitation for the sick and imprisoned. Frank offered a strong hand and a soft shoulder. Frank lived a life that ate the scroll he was divinely commanded to eat, and then from the abundance of his heart, Frank spoke God's holy writ into all our lives. Jesus was once asked by what authority He was doing such things. Jesus simply said, "The baptism of John was from what source, from heaven or from men?" (Matthew 21:25 NASB) The religious leaders refused to answer. So did Jesus. So did Frank, and just like Jesus, Frank just kept ministering and inspired many a young preacher, and one from Westover specifically, to kick down the gates of Hell and bring as many as possible to Jesus Christ.

Frank Hawkins lived as a man of divine authority.

Frank was also a man of righteous anger.

The next two parts of this eulogy are going to be difficult to hear, but Frank treasured these next two characteristics even though sometimes by his own admission he did not want to.

Many believe you cannot be a Christian and be angry. Well, frankly, friends, the need for anger to be restricted from a Christian's life is a lie from the pits of Hell. Jesus was often angry. Jesus blistered religious authority and His own disciples. He struck the unfruitful fig tree and told a raging storm it had better get in line. Many of us believe He upset the money changing tables in the temple not once but twice. He called Herod a sly old fox, reminded Martha in no uncertain terms, "I am the resurrection and the life" (John 11:25 NASB), and said to Simon Peter, "Get behind me Satan!" (Matthew 16:23 NASB) It is Jesus' tenacity that allows the children of God to drink death like water. Righteous anger is a necessary part of the Christian life, but it is a fragile balance between holiness and rage that must be nurtured by the Holy Spirit to a place of healing and maturity.

Paul reminds the Church at Ephesus of David's words from Psalm 4, "Tremble, and do not sin; meditate in your heart upon your bed, and be still. Offer the sacrifices of righteousness, and trust in the Lord." (Psalm 4:4, 5 NASB)

Jesus' half-brother, James, equally advises each member of the Body of Christ, "This you know, my beloved brethren. But everyone must be quick to hear, slow to speak and slow to anger; for the anger of man does not achieve the righteousness of God. Therefore, putting aside all filthiness and all that remains of wickedness, in humility receive the word implanted, which is able to save your souls. (James 1:19–21 NASB)

In light of the tragedies Frank faced in his life, he and I had many a discussion about the anger that was burning inside Frank's gut. Not one time did I ever hear Frank respond to loss like Job who said, "Therefore I will not restrain my mouth; I will speak in the anguish of my spirit, I will complain in the bitterness of my soul. Am I the sea, or the sea monster, that You set a guard over me?... Have I sinned? What have I done to You, O watcher of men? Why have You set me as Your target, so that I am a burden to myself? Why then do You not pardon my transgression and take away my iniquity? For now I will lie down in the dust; and You will seek me, but I will not be." (Job 7:11–12, 20–21 NASB) Frank did feel anguish, and there was bitterness in his soul, but he never testified to me that he felt as though he had become God's target or a burden. He never confessed a deep sin to me nor said that he believed some wrong that he had committed was resulting in punishment from God. Frank never believed these things.

He was angry because of tragedy.

He was angry because of unexpected loss.

Still, Frank's heart was set on being the example of the righteousness of God, so Frank Hawkins waited patiently on the Lord to sustain him.

As Frank did, he healed and matured even more so in Christ, and as a result, the words of Psalm 40 emerged from Frank's once righteously angered soul:

I waited patiently for the LORD;
And He inclined to me and heard my cry.
He brought me up out of the pit of destruction, out of the miry clay,
And He set my feet upon a rock making my footsteps firm.
He put a new song in my mouth, a song of praise to our God;
Many will see and fear
And will trust in the LORD.

How blessed is the man who has made the LORD his trust,
And has not turned to the proud, nor to those who lapse into falsehood.
Many, O LORD my God, are the wonders which You have done,
And Your thoughts toward us;
There is none to compare with You.
If I would declare and speak of them,
They would be too numerous to count.

Sacrifice and meal offering You have not desired;
My ears You have opened;
Burnt offering and sin offering You have not required.
Then I said, "Behold, I come;
In the scroll of the book it is written of me.
I delight to do Your will, O my God;
Your Law is within my heart."

I have proclaimed glad tidings of righteousness in the great congregation;
Behold, I will not restrain my lips,
O LORD, You know.

I have not hidden Your righteousness within my heart;
I have spoken of Your faithfulness and Your salvation;
I have not concealed Your lovingkindness and Your truth from
the great congregation.

You, O LORD, will not withhold Your compassion from me;
Your lovingkindness and Your truth will continually preserve me.
For evils beyond number have surrounded me;
My iniquities have overtaken me, so that I am not able to see;
They are more numerous than the hairs of my head,
And my heart has failed me.
Be pleased, O LORD, to deliver me;
Make haste, O LORD, to help me.

(PSALM 40:1–13 NASB)

It never happens as quickly as we would desire, but God did come perfectly to relieve the anger in Frank's heart, and at the place of Frank's healing and maturity, I witnessed the perfection of Christ's love in my dear friend and brother's heart.

Frank Hawkins became a man of the Messiah's forgiveness.

One November night in this sanctuary during a Bible study, a number of years after Frank's two greatest losses, Frank walked up these steps to a pulpit and said very simply, "I forgive the man who killed my son."

Frank had spoken the word of God from his heart and stood as an example for all of us.

Nothing has changed from that night.

I know not everyone in this room has been healed of hurt yet. Some would rather have me not to say anything at all here today, but from Frank's redeemed and matured heart has emerged perfect love and example. It is one Frank and his Lord call us to walk in. The Messiah's forgiveness is a lonely place. Jesus spent much time there, so did Frank, and both call us to do the same. This brings me to the final quality of Frank he was and exampled for us.

Frank Hawkins was a man of solitude.

Jesus was alone in the wilderness. Jesus was alone in Gethsemane. Jesus was alone on the cross. The Scriptures speak how Jesus would often head out to lonely places and acquaint Himself with sorrow there. Yet no one who encountered Christ with loving welcome was ever moved to do anything but share in His joy. I'm guessing we all feel the same about Frank. He always brought us the joy of the Lord.

Frank and I talked many times about how he loved being around his family and the guys from Kingdom he would go to breakfast with. We had many an amazing Saturday morning in prayer and Bible study, and there is not a single person who went through Frank's Holy Communion line who was not blessed by his gentle smile and willingness to serve our Lord. But Frank and I also talked about the solitude of night he experienced when we all went to our homes and he was alone within his. Frank would tell me how he would look around his home place at the darkness outside and the seeming emptiness within. He would hear the enemy temptingly whisper to him, "Frank, you're all alone." Still, our dear brother never gave the devil a foothold in those moments. Instead, in the silence of solitude, Frank came to experience the silence of God. Frank was still, and he came to know God even more than he already did. It is not in the thunder, or the lightning, or the earthquake where we find God. No... it is in the still small voice that whispers, "What are you doing here, Frank?" God whispered Frank's name within the solitude of Frank's life, and our dear brother always answered.

Right before I left Frank's room last Tuesday, Carol said to Frank, "Dad, do you know who that is at the foot of your bed?" Frank looked at his little girl a little confused as to why she would ask such a question, and he said, "Well, that's Kevin."

I smiled.

Then my dear friend and brother said the final words that I ever heard from him, "I love you, Kevin."

"I love you too, Frank."

Frank Hawkins is the embodiment of the Holy Spirit Who lives within him.

Frank Hawkins is example of Christ's love and forgiveness before us.

There is a calling for each of us to live in the same manner

We got 'er made now, Frank. We love you, too.

May the peace and blessing of our God that rests upon Frank rest upon each of you this day.

Epitaph of Reconciliation:
It's Never Too Late

As death is making its pilgrimage to all of us, we must sanctify the time. It is the moment and not the space in which we are called to live. In the momentary living, we are forever being born by the good news of Christ's reconciling love. Reconciliation both patiently waits for us and lovingly sings to us. It is never too late.

As a boy, exchanges of "I love you" with my Marine, hydraulic-machine-shop-owning father were nonexistent. It wasn't that I didn't love him or he didn't love me. We just didn't say it. Like all of the father-son relationships around me, I would say, "My dad doesn't need to tell me he loves me. I know he does." While my knowledge of my father's love was firmly rooted, the dismissed desire to hear the actual words from his lips was a thinly veiled lie. Every son, even when he knows it, wants to hear from his father, "I love you, Son, and I am very proud of you."

I can say with total honesty and certainty the only time my dad and I told one another "I love you" was when I was growing up after a fight we had. It was in front of my best friend, which heightened my ego, and thus the drama. I said things. Dad said things. I did things. Dad did things. All the while my friend stood big-eyed between us. Somewhere in the midst of the flurry, I ran from the house and into the night. I was too angry to face my dad. I was too embarrassed to face my friend. I did not care whether I saw either of them ever again.

Then while huffing and puffing through my neighborhood, I came across my preacher walking his dog. He could see that I was more than enraged, so he did his very best to try to talk to me. I was so angry that tears were coming to my eyes. My dad was a great guy. My friend was a great guy. My preacher was a great guy. I just couldn't reconcile the night while holding a tempest of teenage rage.

My preacher, with reconciliation on his breath, said, "You have to go home. You have to say, sorry. You have to say, 'I love you.'"

My preacher was right and I was so wrong. I headed immediately home, where my friend's dad had already picked him up. Dad was waiting in the kitchen.

Neither of us tried to explain. Neither of us tried to justify. We both looked at each other and said, "I'm so sorry. I love you."

Until the first year of my marriage, that night was the only time my dad and I told one another "I love you."

Fast forward eight years.

I'm now twenty-three years old and newly married. It's the early nineties and my dad is in the midst of major heart problems. He is facing a very modern surgery, and no doctor in Morgantown, West Virginia, is qualified to perform the procedure. Fortunately, Pittsburgh was an hour up the road, so my entire family and I headed north to save my dad's life.

The morning of the surgery, doctor upon doctor came into our room explaining this and explaining that, all of which I did not understand. Even without the medical and anatomical terms I was unfamiliar with, the sheer emotion of the chance of losing my dad was fogging my brain.

One final doctor came into the room and said, "Good morning. I'm Dr. So-and-so; I will be observing the surgery this morning and poised to save you, Mr. Cain. If your family ever sees me again it will be because you've died and I have had to save you. Do you have any questions?"

I had a lot of questions.

Yet the only thing I could think of was that the only time I had ever told my dad I loved him was after a stupid fight between father and teen-age son. There was no way I was going to allow my dad to be gurneyed out for surgery and me miss the chance to say "I love you." I know for some "I love you" flows like water, but not in most father-to-son relationships in Appalachian homes.

At this point, I was a grown man.

At this point, I was preaching the Gospel of Jesus Christ.

At this point, the nurses and transporters came into the room and said, "Are you ready, Mr. Cain?"

I pushed from the wall upon which I was leaning, took my dad by the hand, and said, "I love you, Dad."

He looked up at me and said, "I love you too, buddy."

Then they rolled him away down a long, white, sanitized corridor.

We waited unsettled.

He made it through the surgery just fine.

That next Sunday, my wife and I attended our home church in our stomping grounds of Westover. In most small Appalachian churches, there used to be a time in the service called "Joys and Concerns." It was a time for parishioners to stand and give a testimony or a prayer request. Then, after everyone had sufficiently offered, the preacher would offer the *Pastoral Prayer*.

The liturgist stood behind the lectern and said, "Does anyone have a joy or concern this morning?"

I stood up and simply said, "I do. This past week my dad had heart surgery. My family and I thank all of you for all the prayers, concerns, and well wishes. Dad is doing just fine and will be up and at 'em soon. I just want to say one thing, though. Through all of this I've realized that we have to make the most of every moment God gives us. If we need to forgive, then we should forgive. If we need to reconcile, then we need to reconcile. Through all of these, I've learned ..."

It's never too late to be a dad.

It's never too late to be a son.

A Thought as You Step Back onto Life's Carousel ...

My great-grandfather lived his life as a circuit-riding preacher. He offered some advice to my maternal grandmother who, in turn, offered the advice to her daughter, my mother. My mother has offered the advice to me: *Pray for a peaceful moment in which to die.* With this Godly counsel in mind, I have always done my very best to offer life in the midst of death. Peace in the midst of passing is the greatest beauty to be found.

With his sons circling his deathbed and with honest blessings for them flowing from his lips, the Biblical patriarch, Jacob, shows us the way to the beauty of passing's peace:

> *"When Jacob finished charging his sons, he drew his feet into the bed and breathed his last, and was gathered to his people."*
> *(Genesis 49:33 NASB)*

Comfort one another with these words.